The New Zealand Economy

The New Zealand Economy

An Introduction

Ralph Lattimore and Shamubeel Eaqub

with contributions by Gary Hawke and Philip McCann

AUCKLAND UNIVERSITY PRESS

First published 2011

Auckland University Press
University of Auckland
Private Bag 92019
Auckland 1142
New Zealand
www.auckland.ac.nz/aup

ISBN 978 1 86940 489 5

National Library of New Zealand Cataloguing-in-Publication Data
Lattimore, Ralph G.
The New Zealand economy : an introduction / by Ralph Lattimore
and Shamubeel Eaqub.
Includes index.
ISBN 978-1-86940-489-5
1. New Zealand—Economic policy. 2. New Zealand—
Economic conditions—21st century. I. Eaqub, Shamubeel. II. Title.
330.993—dc 22

Cover design: Carolyn Lewis

Printed by Printlink Ltd, Wellington

Contents

List of tables

List of graphs

Preface

This book introduces the structure and performance of the New Zealand economy. It does so by interpreting key data series on the economy in a historical and global context. The book is designed to follow on from an earlier series (*The New Zealand Macroeconomy*) produced from 1991 to 2004 by Paul Dalziel and Ralph Lattimore.

The book focuses, first, on how the globalisation of the world economy over the last 30 years has transformed the New Zealand economy. Over this period, developing countries have grown more rapidly than high-income countries and become more embedded in global supply chains. At the forefront of these developments has been a set of emerging economies, including China, India and Vietnam, which have grown strongly in recent years. These changes in the global economic landscape are significantly influencing New Zealand's performance and prospects.

The book focuses, second, on the continuing effects of the 2007 Global Financial Crisis (GFC). The ensuing recession and the difficulties associated with finding an exit strategy from the massive fiscal and monetary stimuli have left world financial markets in an uncertain state. In this environment, the book pays particular attention to capital and financial markets in New Zealand and overseas.

This book is targeted at two potential audiences. It is designed as an introductory text on the performance of the New Zealand economy for school and university students. It is also aimed at those who want a pocket guide to the New Zealand economy.

New Zealand has developed a reputation in recent decades for what many people consider to be 'continuous reform'. The international trade policy expert Professor Razeen Sally is of the view (Sally, 2009) that New Zealand is one of only two countries in the world that have the capacity to deal politically with continuous reform (the other being Australia). That is a major strength for the nation but it puts a great onus on advisers and analysts in the private and public sectors, and the public at large, to understand how the economy is performing and why. This book is designed to help inform necessary debates on policy changes.

Because it is an introductory text, the book does not go into depth on most economic issues. However, two guest case studies are included which explore issues involved in the process of technological and geographic change in more detail, but in a way that makes these issues accessible to general readers. The first study, by Professor Gary Hawke, explores technical change and related productivity improvements. Technical change is often misunderstood, which leads to incoherent approaches to research and science policy. The second study, by Professor Philip McCann, introduces the new topic of economic geography. This area of research is gaining in popularity at present as it attempts to explain drivers of city and regional economic growth patterns based on productivity improvements unleashed especially by modern communications technology. Both case studies are designed as introductory resources for further exploration in these two important areas of economic research.

The authors owe a large intellectual debt to a number of economists who have contributed to this book through their journal articles and private conversations. Foremost amongst these are Edward Leamer's review article in the *Journal of Economic Perspectives* (2007), the report of the World Bank's Growth Commission (2008), Michael Bordo's study of New Zealand's exposure to the Global Financial Crisis (2009), Kym Anderson's prodigious work on world trade distortions, Michael Reddell and Cathy Sleeman's work on New Zealand recessions (2008), and Carmen Reinhart and Kenneth Rogoff's momentous study of financial crises (2008). Martin Wolf's column in the *Financial Times* has been unparalleled in bringing important research on global finance to the fore over the past three years.

The members of the Advisory Committee on Economic Statistics at Statistics New Zealand have contributed ideas in many ways. Special mention must also be made of contributions by Iris Claus, Adolf Stroombergen, Peter Lloyd, Javier Reyes, Martina Garcia, Przemyslaw Kowalski and Raed Safadi.

The Reserve Bank of New Zealand and Statistics New Zealand contributed valuable data for the book and we are very grateful to them for allowing us to use that data here. Oxford University Press kindly agreed to allow us to use selected material from the 2004 edition of Dalziel and Lattimore's *The New Zealand Macroeconomy: Striving for Sustainable Growth with Equity*.

Thanks are also due to all the staff at Auckland University Press, and two anonymous referees, for their assistance and helpful suggestions.

The data used to construct the graphs and tables in the book, which will be updated quarterly, are available to readers at http://sites.google.com/site/eaqubs/

We apologise in advance for any errors or omissions in the manuscript and we welcome any comments readers might like to send.

Ralph Lattimore (Ralph.Lattimore@yahoo.com)
Shamubeel Eaqub (Shamubeel.Eaqub@nzier.org.nz)

Abbreviations

AIG	American Insurance Group
ANZCERTA	Australia New Zealand Closer Economic Relations Trade Agreement
ANZSIC	Australian and New Zealand Standard Industrial Classification system
APEC	Asia-Pacific Economic Cooperation
CFR	core funding ratio
CPI	consumer price index
DSIR	Department of Scientific and Industrial Research
EEC	European Economic Community
EU	European Union
FTE	full-time equivalent
GATT	General Agreement on Tariffs and Trade
GDP	gross domestic product
GFC	Global Financial Crisis
GST	goods and services tax
ICTs	information and communications technologies
IMF	International Monetary Fund
NAFTA	New Zealand Australia Free Trade Agreement (or North American Free Trade Agreement)
OCR	Official Cash Rate
OECD	Organisation for Economic Co-operation and Development
OPEC	Organization of Petroleum Exporting Countries
PTA	Policy Targets Agreement
R&D	research and development
RBNZ	Reserve Bank of New Zealand
SDRs	Special Drawing Rights
UN	United Nations
WTO	World Trade Organization

1 Introduction to the New Zealand economy

INTRODUCTION

New Zealand is a small open economy with an income level that places it among the richest countries in the world. As an open economy, New Zealand has vital links with the rest of the world via trade, migration flows, historic, diplomatic, sporting and cultural affiliations, and market connections in products, components and financial flows. These connections have been developing since the late 18th century, when regular transport and communication links were established with other economies. And as a small economy, with a population of 4.5 million, New Zealand is strongly influenced by offshore market performance through such global ties.

Nevertheless, New Zealand's institutions and governments do influence its economic destiny. The strength of the global connections, in one sense, limits the country's freedom of action as compared to very large economies such as those of the United States, Japan, China and Germany. Yet, in another sense, New Zealand has greater freedom of action than these large countries. Decisions can be taken nimbly; our actions tend to have small effects internationally and are less likely to draw the attention of other countries.

1

MEASURING THE ECONOMY

A convenient starting point from which to discuss the structure and performance of the New Zealand economy is with a key indicator of overall economic activity – gross domestic product (GDP). GDP is useful in explaining employment and inflation. It is also useful in comparing economic activity levels between countries because GDP numbers are prepared on a standardised basis according to United Nations guidelines.

This aggregate indicator provides us with a snapshot of various aspects of the economy, but it needs to be clearly understood. GDP is not a complete measure. It is an estimate of the total value of final goods and services produced in the New Zealand economy over a particular time period, say a year. However, GDP does not measure people's wellbeing, happiness or wealth. In economics, there are various measures of performance or economic welfare but they are beyond the scope of this introductory book. GDP is discussed here because it is a reasonably straightforward and widely available measure of economic activity. While it tends to capture broad trends in economic activity and consumer welfare, GDP is not a perfect indicator.

Graph 1.1 illustrates GDP in New Zealand since 1970 on a per person basis expressed in real terms – that is, with the rate of price inflation removed so that GDP is closer to 'concrete' changes in economic activity. Real GDP measures activity using the purchasing power of a base year. The vertical axis of the graph measures real GDP per capita in New Zealand dollars using 1995/96 prices in the calculation. In 1970, real GDP per capita was around $19,000, and in 2010 it was around $31,000 – an increase of 63 per cent over the period. This increase in real GDP per capita is caused by two factors: the increased production of goods and services (often via productivity improvements); and the availability of additional resources (human and physical). However, real GDP per capita has not increased smoothly. Analysis of the dips in the graph reveals much about New Zealand's economy, as these recessions often changed its path. We discuss the largest downturns below.

Graph 1.1 **Real gross domestic product per capita, quarterly, 1970–2010**

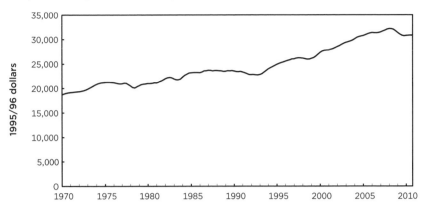

Source: Statistics NZ
Gross domestic product data is sourced from the following:
　1934–1977: McDermott and Hall (2009)
　1977–1987: Statistics NZ, SNBQ.S2SZT
　1987–current: Statistics NZ, SNCQ.S1RB01S
Population data is derived from:
　1934–1991: Statistics NZ, de facto population, DPEQ.SBEC
　1991–current: Statistics NZ, resident population, DEPQ.SDAC

In 1973/74, the world price of oil rose from US$2 per barrel to US$10 per barrel when the Organization of Petroleum-Exporting Countries (OPEC) cartel forged a consensus that enabled them to restrict oil exports following the Arab–Israeli war. New Zealand imported most of its oil at this time and the 1970s oil price hikes caused New Zealanders' cost of living and business's production costs to increase rapidly. Real GDP per capita stopped rising.

The government partially offset the effects of rising oil prices in the early 1970s by borrowing offshore. But it eventually exhausted its credit lines. Without this support, real GDP per capita eventually fell in 1978 and 1979. OPEC export quotas were tightened again in 1979, causing oil prices to surge and deepen New Zealand's economic problems. The decline in GDP from 1978 to 1979 is called a recession. The recession of the late 1970s caused downward pressure on living standards, employment, investment, the exchange rate and a range of other indicators that will be discussed in later sections of the book.

One of the most complex recessions was the stagnation in real GDP per capita from 1985 until the early 1990s. In 1984, the newly elected Labour government faced a foreign exchange crisis and chose to radically reform economic policy from a *command and control* economy towards a more *market-based* economy. This included withdrawing subsidies, floating the exchange rate and moving towards more flexible labour market policies. The policy changes caused a severe dislocation of economic activity as resources moved between sectors to accommodate the new market environment. Real GDP per capita only resumed growth in 1993.

In 1997, the Asian Financial Crisis adversely affected the economic performance of South Korea, Thailand, Taiwan, the Philippines and Indonesia. These are important markets for New Zealand exports and the crisis caused export demand to fall. Because export demand is an important component of total demand in New Zealand, the economy again went into recession.

Over the summer of 2007/08, major dairy farming regions in New Zealand experienced a drought. This is an unusual event in the Waikato and Bay of Plenty. Dairy production and exports fell, along with farmer expenditure on inputs. The drought coincided with the Global Financial Crisis (GFC). During the GFC there was a partial breakdown in trust between major global banks, which threatened the world's payments systems. Investors' appetite for financial risk was severely reduced. The crisis was initially felt in housing markets around the world, which had become increasingly unaffordable. The northern hemisphere GFC and significant interest rate increases by the Reserve Bank of New Zealand (RBNZ) provided the triggers for adjustments in the New Zealand housing market and household consumption. Housing construction declined from late 2007 through to late 2009 and property prices fell by 7 per cent over the same period. Household consumption slowed through 2008 and early 2009. These influences show up in the fall in real GDP per capita in 2008. Much of the world economy (including New Zealand) is still dealing with this correction in house and property prices and the aftermath of the financial crisis. The effects on New Zealand are further discussed in Chapter 7.

There appear to be two distinct phases in real GDP per capita growth over the period 1970–2010: slower economic growth (shallow upward trend) from 1970 to the early 1990s; and faster growth (steeper upward trend) from the early 1990s to 2010. Part of this improving growth rate may be due to the package of economic reforms that was initiated in 1984. However, changes in the market environment caused by globalisation and the rise of the Asian economies, discussed in Chapter 3, probably also had a significant effect on the growth rate of real GDP per capita. Significant increases in household debt funded by the savings of foreigners, discussed in Chapter 6, are also likely to have played a part.

KEY GDP DRIVERS

The brief discussion above suggests a number of key drivers that influence real GDP. The first driver is population. The working population contributes directly to national output through employment and the total population also influences the final demand for goods and services in the economy. The natural increase in the population is usually smooth but net migration is quite variable, Graph 1.2.

Graph 1.2 **Population growth and net migration contribution, 1970–2010**

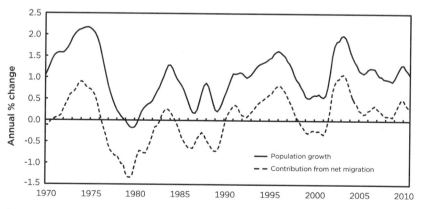

Source: Statistics NZ
Population data as per Graph 1.1
Net migration data: Statistics NZ, ITMQ.SPZNA

The New Zealand population growth rate has averaged 1.4 per cent per annum since 1950. The natural increase in population (births less deaths) is fairly stable. However, migration causes considerable variation in population growth over time. In 2001, population growth was just below 1 per cent and net migration was minus 10,000 persons per year. In the following year, net migration rose to 40,000, boosting the population growth rate to 2 per cent. This led to a significant increase in household spending on goods and services and a construction boom. Real GDP per capita rose steeply over this period.

World prices of New Zealand exports and imports also affect GDP growth. As discussed earlier, oil prices and other import price rises cause GDP per capita to grow more slowly or even decrease. In contrast, rising world prices for New Zealand exports tend to increase real GDP per capita.

Graph 1.3 **Real oil price, 2008 SDR prices, 1970–2010**

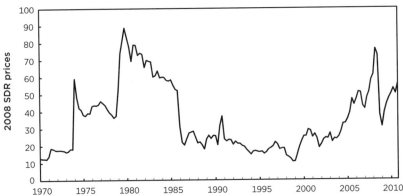

Source: DataStream
UK US$ Brent crude oil price: DataStream, UKI76AAZA
US CPI: DataStream, USCONPRCE
USD to SDR: DataStream, USI.SA

The world oil price has been quite volatile on occasions since 1970, as can be seen in Graph 1.3. The international price of oil is expressed in real Special Drawing Rights (SDRs) in this graph. SDRs are calculated by the International Monetary Fund (IMF) and are comprised of a market basket of major currencies – US dollars, euro, yen, pounds, etc. This currency index removes potential distortions from any one currency's relative strength or weakness in a particular period.

The import and export price effects are combined in a single indicator called the terms of trade, Graph 1.4. The terms of trade measures the ratio of New Zealand export prices to import prices. Let's take an example from the early 1970s. Over the period 1971–73, the prices for New Zealand exports, particularly meat, rose sharply. The terms of trade rose to record-high levels. Real GDP per capita also rose sharply, reflecting this rise in export prices and the terms of trade, Graph 1.1.

This rise in the prices for meat and other agricultural commodities in the early 1970s was caused by the conjunction of a number of weather, market and policy factors. Meat prices rose, mainly because of a shortage of animal feed. An El Niño weather pattern caused anchovies to drift away from the Peruvian coast, which in turn caused a shortage of fishmeal for animal feed. Droughts in the USSR, North America and Australia further compounded the feed shortage. In the policy sphere, the Soviet government decided to maintain their cattle numbers by importing animal feedstuffs (rather than adopt their usual drought policy of slaughtering cattle, which would have dampened prices). Given the size of its cattle industry, Soviet grain imports rose very significantly from the West. The result of all these factors was a temporary 'world food crisis'.

The 1971–73 agricultural commodity price boom did not last. Meat prices fell back to more normal levels, causing the terms of trade to fall in 1974. Coincidentally, OPEC raised oil prices in the same year and one of our major export markets, the United Kingdom, joined the protectionist European Economic Community (EEC). The combined effect of falling export prices and rising import prices caused a record fall in New Zealand's terms of trade – to its lowest level since the Great Depression.

However, real GDP per capita did not fall immediately after the fall in the terms of trade. In fact, it kept rising through 1975. This delayed reaction was caused by New Zealand government policy changes that increased foreign borrowing to buffer the terms of trade shock on GDP. Consequently, real GDP per capita did not fall in line with the 1974 terms of trade decline for some years – until the foreign borrowing limits were reached.

This lag raises another important feature of real GDP fluctuations. New Zealand policy actions are influenced by world market conditions and by domestic business cycles. World market conditions for trade and foreign borrowing set some boundaries for New Zealand economic performance, but domestic policy action can alter the timing of their effects on the domestic economy. Domestic policy can also make the impact of foreign market constraints on New Zealanders worse by dampening necessary market signals. Ultimately, though, a small open economy has to live within its means.

Graph 1.4 **Terms of trade, 1934–2010**

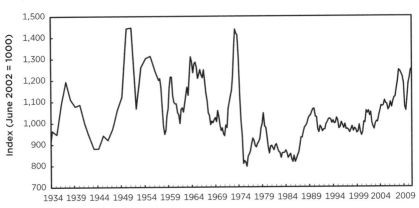

Source: Statistics NZ, RBNZ
1934–1957: Reddell and Sleeman (2008)
1957–current: Statistics NZ, OTPQ.STTZZ5

World capital markets are another important external influence on the New Zealand economy. Because New Zealand borrows foreign savings on a regular basis, interest rates prevailing in world financial markets set a floor (minimum) on interest rates in New Zealand. The effects of

THE NEW ZEALAND ECONOMY

world financial market conditions can be gauged by examining real mortgage interest rates in New Zealand, Graph 1.5. The real interest rate is the nominal or actual rate paid by borrowers minus the inflation rate. Accordingly, the real interest rate is a better measure of the true cost of borrowing and the true return to savers.

Graph 1.5 **Real floating mortgage interest rates, 1920–2010**

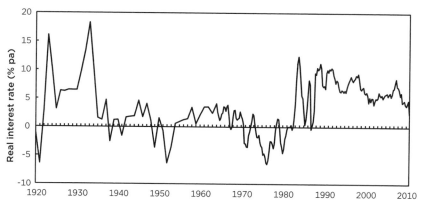

Source: RBNZ, Statistics NZ
1920–1964: Real mortgage rate, Reddell and Sleeman (2008)
1964–current: Nominal mortgage rate, RBNZ, Table B3
1964–current: Consumer price inflation, Statistics NZ, CPIQ.SE9A

In 2010, real interest rates were at their lowest levels for 20 years, Graph 1.5. This was due mainly to the Global Financial Crisis. Central banks around the world slashed interest rates to offset the impact of the GFC on economic activity and jobs. In the United Kingdom and United States, central banks even resorted to 'quantitative easing' (printing money) to try to rescue their economies. Nominal interest rates in many large economies were near zero in 2010 and negative in real terms.

New Zealand interest rates also fell alongside global interest rates. First, the Reserve Bank lowered the Official Cash Rate (OCR) from 8 per cent to 2.5 per cent (around zero in real terms) to stimulate the economy against the recession. Secondly, because New Zealand banks borrow money in foreign money markets, New Zealand mortgage rates followed global interest rates downwards.

The influence of world financial markets on New Zealand real interest rates can be readily appreciated by comparing 2010 to 1984. In 1984, New Zealand experienced a foreign exchange crisis and the economy was performing poorly in many respects. World financial markets viewed New Zealand as a risky place in which to lend. Accordingly, foreign banks were only prepared to lend with a high risk premium. This premium drove real mortgage interest rates up to around 12 per cent (or over 20 per cent in nominal terms). By contrast, real interest rates rarely fall below zero, but this did occur in the mid-1970s, for example. High oil prices led to significant savings by some of the large oil-exporting countries, which were invested in bonds and drove world nominal interest rates below the rate of inflation.

THE STRUCTURE OF THE NEW ZEALAND ECONOMY

Taken as a whole, the economy operates as a circular flow of resources, goods and services. The flow of these items is counterbalanced in the opposite direction by the flow of money from firms to households and back to firms. Goods and services are created by a combination of labour, capital and natural resources. This standard picture of the economy is available in introductory textbooks. Goods (and services) are produced by firms that hire labour and capital services from the owners of these resources – households. Households, in turn, buy final goods from the firms using the income (wages and profits) derived from the sale of their services to the firms.

GDP is an estimate of all this activity and, because the activities are circular, GDP can be measured in three main ways: by income source, by expenditure group and by production group. Examining these approaches to measuring GDP is one way to view the structure of the economy. Bear in mind, however, that each approach to measuring GDP requires large amounts of data. The data is of uneven quality and it is only available with variable time lags due to the timing of Statistics New Zealand surveys. GDP estimated using the three approaches will be different, even though theoretically it should be identical.

Table 1.1 **Gross domestic product by income source,**
year ending March 2010

	$m
Compensation of employees	84,486
Gross operating surplus	80,195
Taxes on production & imports	23,775
Less subsidies	654
Gross domestic product	187,802
Divided by NZ resident population (millions)	4.4
Per capita gross domestic product ($)	43,056

Source: Statistics NZ
National Accounts: Year ended March 2010, Table 1.1

Table 1.1 shows a breakdown of GDP estimated by how much income firms have paid to households for the use of their labour, management services and capital. The two largest categories of income are the compensation of employees (wages and salaries) and the gross operating surplus. The latter item includes the profits from farms and other businesses. New Zealand has a large number of owner-operated firms and the wages of the operator are often counted in the operating surplus of such firms. In the year ending March 2010, the compensation of employees amounted to $84 billion and the gross operating surplus was $80 billion. With adjustments for taxes paid and subsidies received from government, GDP is estimated to have been $188 billion in 2010.

Table 1.2 shows GDP estimated by spending for the same year ending March 2010. Expenditure by households of $110 billion is the largest category, followed by government expenditure of $38 billion. Investment ($35 billion) is the expenditure in New Zealand by households, firms and government on productive goods that are likely to be useful to firms for some years. One thinks of computers which ought to remain current for two or three years or hydro-electric power stations that will have a useful life of many decades. Exports ($52 billion) measures the expenditure by foreign consumers (households and firms) on goods and services produced in New Zealand. This export demand is another important driver of productive activity in New Zealand. Expenditure by New Zealanders on imports has the opposite effect to export demand. Import demand provides goods and services to New Zealand households but, since they are not produced in New Zealand, the value of imports is subtracted from expenditure on GDP. With this adjustment, NZ GDP by expenditure is estimated as $187 billion in the March 2010 year – slightly below the GDP by income group estimate.

Table 1.2 **Gross domestic product by expenditure group, year ending March 2010**

	$m
Consumption	
Private	110,834
Government	38,213
Investment	35,521
Exports	52,424
Less imports	49,690
Gross domestic product	187,302
Divided by NZ resident population (millions)	4.4
Per capita gross domestic product ($)	42,941

Source: Statistics NZ
National Accounts: Year ended March 2010, Table 1.1

The third way to estimate GDP is by measuring the levels of economic activity in the groups of firms (production groups or industries) that make up the economy, Table 1.3. Note that up-to-date data on this measure is not available, so the GDP estimate in Table 1.3 is for the year to March 2007.

Economic activity in each firm is measured by value added. Value added is the gross revenue of a firm less the cost of component parts and other inputs produced by other firms. These inputs will include electricity, paper, pens, diesel, accounting services and a host of other items. The remainder once the cost of inputs has been subtracted is called value added and it consists of the wages, rental payments, interest and profits earned by the firm. In other words, value added has the same items embedded in it as those measured in GDP by income source. The difference is the method of estimation.

Table 1.3 **Gross domestic product by production group, year ending March 2007**

	$m
Market production groups	
Agriculture	7,450
Forestry, logging, fishing & mining	3,362
Manufacturing	23,446
Electricity, gas & water supply	4,502
Construction	8,840
Distribution	23,637
Transport, storage & communication services	11,671
Finance, insurance, property & business services	35,635
Ownership of owner-occupied dwellings	12,671
Community, social & personal services	6,182
Less bank service charges	6,552
Non-market production groups	
Health & community services	9,550
Education	6,885
Central & local government services	7,909
Total production	155,188
Plus GST on production	11,472
Plus import duties	1,668
Gross domestic product	168,328
Divided by NZ resident population (millions)	4.2
Per capita gross domestic product ($)	40,094

Source: Statistics NZ
National Accounts: Year ended March 2010, Table 1.5

Table 1.4 **Industry employment characteristics, 2001**

	FTE	Part-time	With degrees	Maori	Female	Capital/
	(% of total)		(% of sector)			labour index
Primary sector						
Agriculture	7.6	22	2	9	33	61
Forestry	0.6	13	7	37	12	25
Fishing	0.2	13	7	33	12	48
Mining	0.2	7	17	15	10	100
Manufacturing sector						
Food, beverages	3.3	10	3	21	32	22
Textiles, clothing, footwear	1.2	14	3	10	57	10
Wood products	1.1	8	4	21	14	16
Paper, printing, publishing	1.7	18	6	10	37	19
Chemicals, plastics, etc.	1.1	8	6	10	27	29
Non-metallic minerals	0.4	11	10	13	18	19
Basic metals	0.3	5	11	12	11	32
Machinery, metal products	3.7	8	3	9	17	10
Other manufacturing	0.9	14	5	8	23	11
Services sector						
Electricity, water & gas	0.4	7	15	10	29	67
Building, construction	6.4	11	1	12	10	12
Trade, restaurants, hotels	21.6	30	2	9	46	12
Transport, storage	4.1	13	2	13	27	23
Communications	1.3	23	6	13	43	39
Finance, insurance, business	14.6	19	9	7	51	25
Government	4.6	11	11	14	45	15
Education	7.0	31	20	11	69	6
Health	7.6	35	11	10	80	6
Community services	10.0	32	4	13	45	16
Mean		23	5	11	43	

Source: The employment data are obtained from the Population Census undertaken by Statistics New Zealand every five years. The capital/labour ratios are calculated using capital estimates provided in Statistics New Zealand's input–output tables.

The finance, insurance, property and business sector contributed almost $36 billion to GDP in the year to March 2007. This was the largest production group in the economy, contributing around 21 per cent of total GDP. The next largest production group was distribution. Distribution comprises wholesale and retail firms and includes bars, restaurants, motels and hotels, which capture a significant amount of tourist expenditure. Manufacturing was about the same size as distribution, each contributing around 14 per cent of total value added (or GDP).

One of the interesting features of the production structure of the New Zealand economy, for a higher-income country, is the large agricultural (farming) sector. Farming represents 4.4 per cent of total GDP. This is two or three times the size of the farming sectors in many other high-income countries. The New Zealand farm sector is concentrated in the production of animal products (milk and meat), and as a result our largest manufacturing industry is food processing. Animal products usually need more processing before they can be traded internationally. By contrast, the food-processing sector in large agricultural-producing countries such as the United States, Canada and Brazil represents a much smaller share of manufacturing. The large food-processing sector in New Zealand is the result of New Zealand's rather unique pattern of comparative advantages. These are discussed in later chapters.

The various production groups have different production technologies and this is reflected in the composition of their workforces and the ratio of capital equipment they use relative to employee numbers, Table 1.4.

Firms in industries such as electricity, gas and water use large capital inputs (machinery, equipment, dams, etc.) and employ very few workers. Industries such as finance require relatively little capital (office buildings, computers, etc.) but large workforces. The amount of training differs widely between sectors. The education sector requires a large proportion of workers with university degrees while the forestry sector does not – it trains most of its workers on the job. These differences will be discussed in Chapters 5 and 6.

The composition of production groups contributing to a country's GDP changes with economic development because as households get richer they will spend on different products and services. For example, a higher-income country will usually want a relatively larger finance sector than a lower-income country. Accordingly, economic resources are continually on the move from one production group to another. These changes have important implications for people planning careers, investors evaluating opportunities and the government developing research and education policies.

Finally, there are some important measurement issues to deal with. You will notice in Table 1.3 that government activities are grouped as non-market production groups. Many government services are not bought and sold in markets and accordingly there is no market price data available to estimate their contribution to GDP. Central government services are valued at cost. This valuation is most unlikely to be correct but it would simply be too expensive to estimate the true value of government services on a regular basis.

While GDP is the preferred measure of economic activity and a proxy for the standard of living, it has many other limitations. For example, in GDP measurement the cost of an oil spill is not counted but the clean-up is. A country's black economy and unpaid work are not counted. And though factors such as income equality, health, educational attainment and happiness have an important bearing on the actual success of an economy, they are not explicitly captured in GDP either.

CONCLUSION

New Zealand is a small open economy. Being small, it is heavily influenced by global events and forces, but local institutions and government policies are also important drivers of its economic performance. Net migration, commodity prices and interest rates are key influences on the economy.

The level of economic activity is generally measured using gross domestic product (GDP). GDP approximates total income, spending or production in the economy for a period. However, it is not a perfect measure and does not necessarily reflect the health, wealth and happiness of the population.

2 New Zealand's long-term economic performance

INTRODUCTION

Chapter 1 was a general overview of the New Zealand economy with a focus on one indicator of economic performance – gross domestic product (GDP) per capita. This chapter expands to four key indicators which macroeconomists often use to summarise the performance of an economy. They are income per capita, the inflation rate, the unemployment rate and the current account balance. Each of these indicators is discussed in order to give a broad outline of the performance of the New Zealand economy. Subsequent chapters (3 to 8) will look behind these four summary indicators to examine the performance of the economy in more detail.

ECONOMIC HISTORY

We can learn a great deal about how the economy performs by looking closely at moments when markets in New Zealand were subjected to strong domestic or foreign influences. This is in part because the events that have shaped the past (economic crises, food shortages, price spikes or changes in government policy) will very likely also shape the future. Observing the past helps us to understand how social, political and economic behaviour changes in response to crises and this can help us forecast the rates and directions of future economic change.

The Global Financial Crisis (GFC) of 2007, which caused a near-collapse of the banking system in the United States and Europe, is an example of an economic shock. Financial crises threaten the wealth of savers and the ability of households and firms to conduct day-to-day business activities. Financial crises occur quite frequently – almost every decade or so somewhere around the world. Governments have sometimes proven ineffective in countering such crises and indeed are often involved in causing the problems. Understanding past financial and other crises can give us some insight into common causes and potential cures.

NEW ZEALAND'S RELATIVE INCOME PER CAPITA

GDP per capita is an approximation of income per person in an economy. It is often correlated with the standard of living. It is also measured consistently across countries, making international comparisons possible. New Zealand is a relatively wealthy country and it used to have one of the highest levels of GDP per capita. However, currently it is not as rich as either the United States or Australia.

The work of Angus Maddison at the Organisation for Economic Co-operation and Development (OECD) and of other researchers has resulted in time series estimates of income per capita for continents and many countries covering a period of over 1000 years. Income per capita is measured in this research in novel ways (estimating food intake, for example) rather than through the formal estimates of real GDP per capita as described in Chapter 1. These alternative approaches are necessary as we do not have the historical data to use the modern national income accounting approach. Nevertheless, the more basic methods do produce important insights.

One of the conclusions of this research is that average per capita incomes worldwide did not rise at all until the 18th century due to a lack of technological innovation. On the other hand, per capita incomes have risen significantly since 1700 as countries adopted new technology associated with scientific agriculture and the industrial revolution. These results sometimes surprise people who are familiar with the great inventions that occurred in the centuries before that date: one thinks of written language, number systems and mathematics, the wheel, gunpowder, the loom, double-entry book-keeping, wind power and banking as examples. But factors other than inventions are required for economic progress via technological change, for example business, social and political environments conducive to commercialising inventions. Achieving and maximising these environments is the great challenge of economic organisation. Interested readers are encouraged to look at the two case studies at the end of this book, which begin to expand on many of the issues involved in the process of technological change.

New Zealand's per capita income from 1820 to 2009 is illustrated in Graph 2.1. In this graph New Zealand and Australia's average per capita incomes are plotted relative to average per capita income in the United States. When New Zealand's relative per capita income has a value of 1 in the graph it means that per capita incomes were the same in New Zealand as they were in the US.

Prior to 1840, New Zealand had a diverse set of industries. Export industries were built around depletable resources – kauri gum, kauri timber, gold, seal oil, whale oil and some smaller agricultural products. There were industries devoted to producing substitutes for imports (for example, farm machinery, clothing and footwear) and service industries (for example, transport, banking, hotels and retailing) meeting the wants of the resident population. New Zealand and Australian per capita incomes were around 30 per cent of US levels. The US had been settled much earlier and early industrialisation was producing rapid growth.

The first turning point for New Zealand relative per capita incomes came just after 1840. Wool was a highly valued commodity and the expansion of sheep farming from 1840 led per capita incomes in this country to rise – along with Australia – to a peak of 40 per cent above US levels in 1880. Australasia had the highest per capita incomes in the world. This was a remarkable achievement, because the US economy was also growing fast. For example, total US GDP surpassed that of the much more populous and mature economy of China in the 1870s. Both the US and New Zealand had high rates of population growth as a result of strong net migration flows, which boosted total GDP.

Graph 2.1 **New Zealand and Australia GDP per capita relative to US, 5-yearly, 1820–2009**

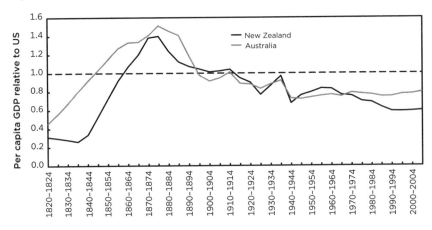

Source: Anderson et al. (2008), Conference Board
1820–1950: Anderson et al. (2008)
1950–current: Conference Board Total Economy Database

The basis of this per capita income growth in New Zealand was the initial availability of the natural grasslands on the east coast of the South Island, but it was also assisted by the application of scientific agriculture techniques developed in Europe. These included selective livestock breeding, grazing systems, plant selection, fertiliser applications and milk testing.

The second half of the 19th century was also characterised by the relatively free global movement of goods, services and migrants – what is called a period of globalisation. For example, trade barriers to the UK market were lowered mid-century with the removal of the Corn Laws (wheat import tariffs), and a number of other countries (including Japan) opened or reopened their economies to international commerce.

In 1882, on-board refrigeration was introduced on New Zealand overseas shipping routes and the agricultural sector was revolutionised once more by access to UK markets for meat and dairy products. The new export triumvirate – wool, meat and dairy – helped keep New Zealand near the top of the world real per capita GDP stakes for the next 70 years. The continued growth of these exports required the development of competitive processing industries for dairy and meat products as well as continuing market access efforts by industry and government. Multinational firms were prominent in these initiatives. Work on trade relations was significant because the globalisation that began in the 19th century came to an abrupt halt with the declaration of war in 1914. Yet it was no accident that New Zealand agricultural exports continued to flourish throughout the volatile 1920s and the Great Depression. Commonwealth preferences, nurtured by New Zealand politicians and business leaders, aided New Zealand's economic performance.

The US economy continued to grow very quickly after 1880, stimulated by the commercialisation of technological advances in internal combustion engines, electricity and communications. Per capita incomes in the US grew faster than in New Zealand (and Australia), so that by 1915 New Zealand had fallen below parity with the US. After a drop in relative New Zealand per capita incomes in the 1920s, relative incomes improved towards parity from the 1930s to the period leading up to World War II. Thereafter, New Zealand's relative income fell to between 70 and 80 per cent of US levels through the 1950s and early 1960s. From around 1965, New Zealand began a long decline vis-à-vis the US. New Zealand per capita incomes also began to decline relative to Australia from around 1975.

This relative post-World War II decline in New Zealand per capita incomes had a number of causes. The world economy opened up to a new era of globalisation after 1945, but New Zealand remained inwardly focused.

The new globalisation was due to the development of international supply chains based on economies of scale in component manufacture, outsourcing and offshoring. Supply chains also became longer as tasks became more specialised. This involved European countries, the US and emerging economies. Japan and Germany were prime movers with their reconstruction activities.

One of the efficiencies gained in this process was the mobilisation of low-productivity farm labour to higher-productivity employment in industry. This shift disadvantaged New Zealand in three ways. First, New Zealand did not have much low-productivity farm labour to reallocate because labour productivity had been raised in New Zealand agriculture decades before; and second, the small size of the New Zealand market meant that economies of scale were difficult to achieve outside food processing. The third reason was New Zealand's industry policy, which remained rigid. New Zealand (like Australia) refused to dismantle its protection of the manufacturing sector against imports when the General Agreement on Tariffs and Trade (GATT) was formed in 1947. It would not do so partly as a protest against the decision of many original GATT members to relax import restrictions on all products except those originating in the agricultural sector.

However, New Zealand quickly realised that this standoff in the GATT was not in the country's best long-term economic interests and that the country had little hope of changing the situation. New Zealand import protection was temporarily reduced in the 1950s and again in the 1970s only to be reversed under lobbying pressure from manufacturers (Rayner and Lattimore, 1991). This protectionist policy insulated many manufacturing industries from global competition. As a result, many firms did not innovate and invest to follow global productivity trends.

One example of inefficient industrial development was motor vehicle assembly from imported components. When the general car tariff of 25 per cent was finally removed in 1997 the major car companies closed their assembly operations in New Zealand and the GDP contribution of the motor vehicle industry halved over the next year. The industry contribution subsequently rose again as vehicle component manufacturers and related companies adapted to the new policy environment. Some firms even became competitive internationally and began exporting.

The economic reform process that accelerated after 1984 resulted in more efficient resource use in many sectors of the economy, just as it did in the motor vehicle industry after 1997. The move away from import substitution (relaxing import restrictions), by allowing resources to move from unproductive to more productive activities, probably also assisted in halting the decline in per capita incomes in New Zealand relative to the US. From 1990, New Zealand's standing appears to have improved slightly relative to the US.

PRICE INFLATION

Inflation is a general rise in the price level. If some prices fall and others rise, inflation will occur when the rises outweigh the falls. Unanticipated inflation imposes a cost on households and firms by making it more difficult for them to plan their activities. If prices are rising rapidly, households will spend rather than save, as a dollar saved today will buy less tomorrow. If prices are falling sharply, then households will save rather than spend.

One way to measure inflation is to use an index of consumer prices – the consumer price index (CPI). The rate of inflation in New Zealand on this measure is illustrated in Graph 2.2.

Graph 2.2 **Consumer price inflation, 1916–2010**

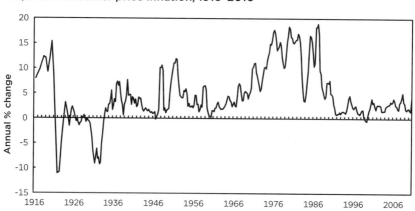

Source: Statistics NZ. CPIQ.SE9A

The end of World War I in 1918 was marked by successive shortages and gluts that caused global price volatility. This volatility was seen also in New Zealand because the New Zealand currency was fixed to the UK pound. With the onset of the Great Depression in 1929, prices generally fell by over 10 per cent, in a process called deflation, Graph 2.2. In 1934 the New Zealand government took control of monetary policy away from the private banks and gave it to the Reserve Bank of New Zealand, with its sole right to issue currency. Over the next 35 years the inflation rate stabilised between zero and 7 per cent, except for a brief period after World War II when price levels rose by over 10 per cent due to shortages of materials and pent-up demand caused by wartime price controls. Additionally, New Zealand experienced a wool export boom in the early 1950s caused by a surge in demand during the Korean War. The increase in export receipts flowed through into consumer incomes, increased demand and prices.

Thereafter, price rises settled down into a 2 to 5 per cent range until the late 1960s. The global price stability experienced from 1945 till the late 1960s is part of the reason this period is often called a 'golden age'. Economic growth was at high levels, international commerce was opening up and inflation was under control. During this period, New Zealand and many other countries had signed on to a fixed exchange rate system administered by the newly created International Monetary Fund (IMF) in 1945 (the Bretton Woods Agreement). The monetary anchor for this IMF system was the US guarantee that it would sell gold at US$35 per ounce to the central banks of participating countries in return for participants agreeing to fix their exchange rates, directly or indirectly, to the US dollar. The payoff to the US from this system was that it encouraged the use of its currency in global commerce and its use in other countries as foreign exchange reserves – the US Treasury could print dollars for a fraction of a cent and other countries would buy and hold them for a dollar. This payoff is called seignorage.

Nevertheless, there were signs early on that the political commitment to the fixed exchange rate system might not be sustained. As early as 1958 the US authorities were forced to fend off an attempt by the French government to call on US gold reserves. In 1969 further pressure came on the international monetary system. The fiscal cost of the Vietnam War to the US was growing and the US government printed money to such an extent that its additional spending caused domestic inflation. US inflation led to inflation in other countries, including New Zealand, because the fixed exchange rates were in force. The pressure on the US became so great that in 1971 President Nixon withdrew US commitment to the gold anchor and in effect the world was on a floating exchange rate system.

As described in Chapter 1, many agricultural commodity prices rose sharply in the early 1970s, which increased the money supply in New Zealand and caused inflation to rise. The New Zealand dollar was revalued upwards against the US dollar a number of times to offset the inflationary effect. At one point the exchange rate was US$1.44 per NZ$1. Then, when oil prices rose sharply in 1974 and 1979, the New Zealand government decided to increase the money supply in an attempt to hold up living standards until oil prices fell again. Oil prices did eventually fall in 1986 (Graph 1.3, p. 6), but in the meantime inflation rose to over 15 per cent.

New Zealand decided not to float its currency following the 1971 breakdown in the Bretton Woods Agreement. Instead the exchange rate became the subject of government direction. The New Zealand dollar was held artificially high during the latter part of the 1970s.

In a desperate attempt to keep the inflation rate down, the government introduced wage, price and interest rate controls in 1981, with a resulting fall in the CPI, Graph 2.2. However, when price controls are introduced, the consumer price index becomes an inexact measure of true inflation because people find ways of circumventing pricing regulations. When the controls were rescinded after 1984 the CPI rose again to over 15 per cent and remained there while the money supply continued to grow.

In 1989 a new monetary policy was introduced that more effectively constrained growth in the money supply. The Reserve Bank was given statutory authority to control inflation under the Reserve Bank of New Zealand Act 1989. After some initial credibility problems, the Reserve Bank managed to reduce the inflation rate to below 5 per cent. It has remained below this figure ever since, except for brief periods. The current monetary policy regime is explained further in Chapter 7.

UNEMPLOYMENT

Employment is a means to support yourself and your family in the modern economy. When the economy is going well, employment is high and unemployment low; when the economy is struggling, the opposite occurs. The unemployment rate is a barometer of economic health.

The unemployment rate is the proportion of working-age people who cannot find a job. The rate goes down when business activity is brisk and unemployed people have skills that are marketable in the expanding economy. The rate goes up during economic downturns.

Graph 2.3 **Unemployment rate, 1921–2010**

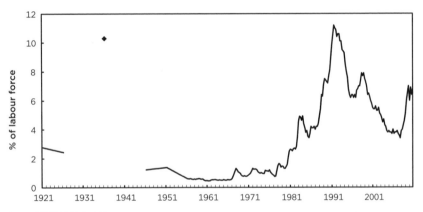

Source: RBNZ, Statistics NZ
1921–1986: Reddell and Sleeman (2008)
1986–current: HLFQ.S1F3S
Consistent data not available in the 1926-1945 period

During the Great Depression the unemployment rate in New Zealand rose to over 10 per cent. This caused enormous hardship, but it was much lower than peak unemployment rates in, for example, Germany (45 per cent) and the US (25 per cent). World War II drew a great many males into the armed forces, and women often replaced men in traditional occupations (a policy that was reversed once soldiers returned after the war). The unemployment rate immediately after the war was less than 2 per cent.

Employment policy from the Great Depression until 1984 involved not just setting wages but also some job creation. People who found themselves unemployed might be assigned jobs in the Forest Service, Post Office or the Railways, for example. As a result, the unemployment rate often sank below 1 per cent in the period up until the late 1960s. Ministers of Labour would joke that they knew all the unemployed on a first-name basis.

In the period from 1945 to 1984 one of the side effects of the import substitution policy was that the demand for university-educated workers was not increasing in line with the technological advances being made in the global economy. The proportion of school-leavers going on to tertiary training institutions was low by international measures. This meant that the labour force was not well suited to deal with the opening up of the economy following the 1984 economic reforms.

With the corporatisation and privatisation of government employment 'sinks' as well as cuts to import protection for the manufacturing sector, unemployment rose steadily from 1984 to reach a new peak in 1991. Thereafter, the unemployment rate fell to around 6 per cent until the recession following the Asian Financial Crisis drove it back up to the 8 per cent level. Unemployment fell to the 3 to 5 per cent range after 2000 until the economy was again hit by recession in 2008.

THE CURRENT ACCOUNT

The current account balance measures many of the transactions across New Zealand's borders. It captures the value of imports and exports, and also some money flows. Conceptually, the current account measures the difference between a nation's savings and its investments. If investment exceeds savings, then we have to borrow as a nation from overseas. Persistent current account deficits, as New Zealand has sustained, indicate an economy with low domestic savings relative to its investment needs.

As seen in Chapter 1, the transactions made in the economy are captured by the estimates of gross domestic product expressed in New Zealand dollars. These estimates are part of the system of national accounts. Some of these transactions were originally conducted in foreign currencies and this subset of receipts and payments is monitored separately.

Imports add to the availability of many raw materials, products and services in the country and accordingly make an important contribution to domestic consumption – they contribute to our living standards. Imports also ensure that best practice technology is available to New Zealand firms so that they can remain competitive on a global basis. Imports of foreign savings ensure that New Zealand investors have access to the finance they require for their project plans.

Imports have another benefit in New Zealand's small domestic market environment. Successful New Zealand firms often grow to the point where they have a very high market share in the economy. In the absence of a liberal import regime, such firms would tend to dominate the local market. In particular, they would have the market power to ration supplies and push prices up. This is the natural strategy of a monopolist. Such firms are constrained in these actions when importers are able to operate freely in the New Zealand market. Accordingly, imports complement the activities of the Commerce Commission in ensuring that New Zealand markets remain competitive.

The price the economy pays for these imports is exports. You can think of this in terms of the foreign currency required to pay for the imports or you can think about how many logs need to be exported to pay for an imported Toyota. Accordingly, a balance is required between exports and imports, and a special statistical account is prepared regularly to track all these international transactions. Though it is called the balance of payments, it encompasses only international payments into and out of the economy.

Imports of goods and services do not have to be balanced by an equal value of exports each year because imports of foreign savings (capital inflows) provide foreign currency as well. However, foreign borrowing adds to the foreign debt of an economy and there are financial constraints on that process, discussed in Chapter 6.

The balance of payments account consists of two parts: the current account and the capital account. The current account includes transactions associated with inflows and outflows of goods (for example, kiwifruit, oil and diggers), services like education, international transport and consulting, and income flows such as the interest on New Zealand's foreign debt and dividends from New Zealand's foreign investments. The capital account balances the current account by recording all international transactions that involve the sale or purchase of assets. It will be discussed in more detail in Chapter 6.

The accounts are prepared using standard double-entry book-keeping. In theory, then, net inflows in one account will equal net outflows in the other account – i.e. the overall balance of payments is always zero. If the balance on the current account for a particular year is negative, the balance on the capital account must be positive and equal in magnitude. In practice, however, there are large gaps in this accounting, in part because capital transactions are more difficult to identify. Accordingly, Statistics New Zealand uses an 'errors and omissions' line to account for this problem.

The New Zealand current account balance has almost always been in deficit since 1970. We tend to import more goods and services than we export and we have to make payments on a lot of foreign liabilities. The current account position is often measured relative to GDP because GDP reflects the economy-wide income level and, indirectly, the creditworthiness of the economy.

Over the period 1950 to 1970 the current account deficit hovered between a surplus of 4 per cent of GDP and a deficit of 5 per cent, Graph 2.4. However, the deficit increased markedly to nearly 15 per cent of GDP in the mid-1970s following the first oil shock. This deficit represented significant foreign borrowing by government to maintain consumption levels and fund 'think big' energy projects.

The current account recovered in the late 1970s from the 15 per cent deficit but the deficit began increasing again from 1980. In the period before 1984 the government followed a fixed exchange rate policy. To underpin this policy it had to maintain foreign exchange reserves with the Reserve Bank so that foreign currency would be available at times when there was excess demand for foreign exchange at the fixed exchange rate. When the current account deficit reached 9 per cent of GDP in 1984, New Zealand's foreign exchange reserves were severely depleted and an exchange rate crisis ensued – the country could no longer continue to finance the large deficits. The government was advised that it needed to devalue immediately but it refused to do so just prior to an election. This decision was reversed under pressure from the new incoming government.

Graph 2.4 **Current account balance, annual, 1951–2010**

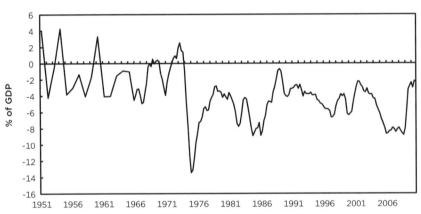

Source: RBNZ, Statistics NZ
1951–1987: Reddell and Sleeman (2008)
1987–current: Statistics NZ, BOPQ.S5R01

The drastic economic reform programme set in motion by the Labour government in 1984 initially resulted in much smaller current account deficits. However, from 1990 to 2002 the current account deficit widened, but remained less than 7 per cent of GDP, Graph 2.4. From 2002, deficits began getting larger as banks imported foreign savings for borrowers speculating in the property market. By the end of 2008, the deficit was almost 9 per cent of GDP again.

THE NEW ZEALAND ECONOMY

When the current account deficit is high the economy can be thought of as 'living beyond its means'; it reflects the shortfall of domestic savings to pay for investment in the economy. Following the Global Financial Crisis we have seen a number of adjustments take place. Savings have generally improved and borrowing has reduced, but so too has investment.

The current account deficit improved quickly in 2009 to less than 3 per cent of GDP. But this improvement was temporary: Australian-owned banks were forced to retain profits in New Zealand to pay some back taxes; and foreign firms in New Zealand had lower profits to remit overseas as a result of the recession. The reduction in the current account deficit is not likely to continue as the economy recovers.

CONCLUSION

The New Zealand economy has become more prosperous over time. However, we have also slipped behind some of our peers, like Australia and the United States, whose real income per capita is higher. The main challenge is to raise productivity – that is, to create more value for every unit of effort. Investment in technology, training and economic efficiency is essential if New Zealand is to catch up.

Inflation is broadly stable in New Zealand. The Reserve Bank is statutorily required to keep inflation under control. A more certain outlook on inflation allows households and businesses to make decisions on spending confidently. In periods of high inflation, it's better to spend rather than save.

New Zealand has tended to run current account deficits. This means that national savings have not usually been sufficient to fund investment, and funds have been borrowed from overseas. New Zealand holds a large stock of foreign liabilities, or obligations to the rest of the world, and this makes it vulnerable. If foreign investors want their funds back, we would have to sell off assets or considerably increase savings, which could slow economic activity, reduce employment and lower our standard of living.

3 Global economic development

INTRODUCTION

Since 1950 the world economy has been transformed and New Zealand's economic relationships have altered in response. Three aspects are discussed in this chapter: globalisation and the rise of Asia; trade policy; and comparative advantages.

While exports from the agricultural sector remain a high proportion, New Zealand's total exports have diversified since 1945 and developed comparative advantages and export competitiveness across a wider range of sectors. The country's export markets have also become more geographically diverse. Part of New Zealand's response to the changing global environment has been a policy shift. New Zealand has lowered its trade barriers to such an extent that it is now one of the most open economies in the world. Its government agencies are also at the forefront of international trade liberalisation efforts.

GLOBALISATION

After the Second World War the world entered a period of renewed globalisation during which international trade, foreign investment and migration increased. The main driver was improvement in technology, which allowed greater trade and interaction over larger distances. As mentioned earlier, increased specialisation has resulted in longer supply chains – that is to say, there are many more steps involved in production processes today. Furthermore, these longer supply chains involve more firms. More tasks are outsourced. The outsourcing is often conducted internationally (offshoring), so that trade may comprise a greater share of production than was previously the case. Technical changes in production systems have been facilitated by modern communications technology (most recently email, the internet and social networking), which ensures that there is a greater flow of ideas. The technology also makes it easier to co-ordinate the activities of firms in the longer supply chains.

The increased movements of ideas, plans, components, goods, money and people were also facilitated by the development of a set of global institutions – the United Nations (UN), the World Bank and regional banks, the International Monetary Fund (IMF), the Organisation for Economic Co-operation and Development (OECD) and its precursor the Marshall Fund, the Asia-Pacific Economic Cooperation organisation (APEC) and the General Agreement on Tariffs and Trade (GATT), which later became the World Trade Organization (WTO).

Post-war globalisation produced a number of rapidly developing economies: first Japan and then South Korea, Taiwan, Indonesia, Brazil, Thailand, Malta, Botswana, Hong Kong, Oman, Malaysia, Singapore and China. These thirteen economies may be referred to as star performers – they grew at over 6 per cent (in real terms) for at least 25 years in a row, meaning average incomes increased almost fourfold. This is two or three times the rate of economic growth of most high-income countries. In the list above, each continent is represented by at least one country but Asia is more heavily represented. And growth in the past two decades mean other countries seem poised to join this 'club' – Vietnam and India, for example.

Globalisation and the rise of emerging economies have had important consequences for the people of the world in terms of the economic opportunities available to individuals and the capacity of governments to improve the distribution of income. In 1950 only 1 billion people lived in fast-growing economies (over 6 per cent real GDP growth per annum) or in high-income countries. In 2007, 4 billion people lived in countries that fall into these two categories.

Globalisation has transformed the global distribution of income, lifting large numbers of people out of poverty, especially in China and in India. It has also increased economic efficiency by drawing hundreds of millions of workers into industries connected to world markets. Globalisation has allowed greater specialisation in production to the benefit of high- and low-income countries alike.

Graph 3.1 **Trade connectedness, centrality index, 1980–2005**

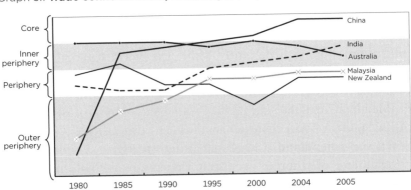

Source: Reyes, Garcia and Lattimore (2009)

Changes in the world economy are evident in measures of world market connections over the past 30 years. Graph 3.1 illustrates trade connectedness using a centrality index. This index measures two factors: how connected a country is to other trading nations and how connected its trading partners are to other trading nations. As measured by the trade connectedness index, a core group of nations that includes Germany, the United States and Japan has traditionally been at the heart of global trade. They are in the 95th percentile of this relative scale. New Zealand, as a small global trader, is on the periphery of world trade connectedness.

THE NEW ZEALAND ECONOMY

China's rise in trade importance has been very rapid on two scores. In 1980, China was in the outer periphery of the trade centrality index but by 1995 its trade connections matched those of the core group. This spectacular increase in trade connectedness is matched by other countries, including South Africa after the trade embargoes were lifted in 1994 – though, unlike China, South Africa is still some way from the core group. On an alternative measure, total trade, China passed Germany in 2009 to become the world's largest exporter. It is also one of the world's largest importers.

As the trade connectedness index for China illustrates, the geography of trade has changed significantly over the past 30 years. Even as global trade relative to world GDP grew from 30 per cent in 1990 to 51 per cent in 2008, the high-income (OECD) countries' share of that trade declined from 73 per cent to 61 per cent. Low-income countries have become much more important in world trade. This shift in global trade has influenced New Zealand's exports and imports. Fast-growing developing countries tend to have a comparative disadvantage in food and this has enabled New Zealand's primary sector to find important new markets in China, other Asian countries and Eastern Europe.

On the other hand, China and other emerging economies have comparative advantages over New Zealand in final manufacturing assembly. By 2007, over 40,000 European Union (EU) companies had established manufacturing subsidiaries in China to commercialise their intellectual property at lower cost. New Zealand's imports reflect the rise of Asian manufacturing. Assembled motor vehicles, computers and whiteware now represent a high proportion of imports.

The changing geographic orientation of New Zealand's export trade is illustrated in Graph 3.2. This graph shows the weighted average distance that New Zealand exports travelled in 2008 compared to 1949. Average distance has halved as the demand for New Zealand exports in Asia has grown relative to Europe and North America.

While New Zealand export market developments have focused on Asia, there have been important developments elsewhere as well. Prior to British entry into the EU in 1973/74, New Zealand primary exports to Europe were concentrated in the UK. Today, France, Germany and Eastern Europe are also major markets.

Graph 3.2 **New Zealand's increased trade with its neighbours, 1949 and 2008**

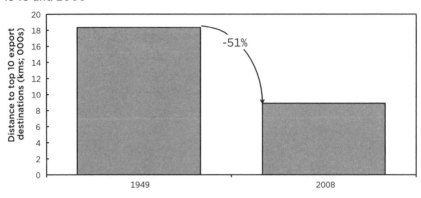

Source: Statistics NZ, CEPII, Pearson Software Consulting
1949 top 10 export destinations: Statistics NZ, 1950 Year Book
2008 top 10 export destinations: Statistics NZ, Monthly Trade Balance, December 2008
Geographic co-ordinates: CEPII geographic database at www.cepii.fr/distance/geo_cepii.xls
Distance calculation: Pearson Software Consulting at http://www.cpearson.com/excel/LatLong.aspx

THE POLITICS OF TRADE, INVESTMENT AND MIGRATION

Most governments continue to restrict full and open globalisation through tariffs or quotas on imports, subsidies for exports, exchange rate manipulations, other regulatory interventions and prohibitions on the movement of goods, services, capital and people between countries. The restrictions are generally lower than they were in 1945 but they have not been eliminated. The policies listed above usually result in economic inefficiency because they inhibit choices for firms and consumers around the world. Specialisation is constrained, living costs are higher than they need be and countries are worse off – they could even be said to be shooting themselves in the foot.

When all (or most) governments maintain these restrictive trade policies the world is also made worse off because export opportunities are reduced and countries cannot take full advantage of their comparative advantages. The world's production possibilities shrink.

As outlined in Chapter 2, New Zealand was seriously disadvantaged by the first GATT agreements after World War II that excluded agricultural and food products from the multilateral trade liberalisation efforts of that organisation. Many developing countries emerged from the removal of colonial ties with new trade restrictions. The result of these policies is illustrated in Table 3.1.

Table 3.1 **Restrictions faced by exporters abroad, 2001–04**

Trade restrictiveness indices, 2001–04			
	Agriculture & food	Other manufactures	All tradables
World	37	10	14
High-income countries	35	10	13
Middle-income countries	39	10	14
Low-income countries	37	12	18
New Zealand	37	12	21

Source: Kee, Nicita and Olarreaga (2006)

As shown in this table, exporters of food and agricultural products face higher trade restrictions than exporters of other manufactured products. Furthermore, middle- and low-income countries apply somewhat higher import barriers than high-income countries.

The restrictions faced by exporters shown in Table 3.1 refer to the period 2001–04. The situation regarding import restrictions on food and agricultural products was worse prior to the Uruguay GATT Round in 1986. This was the first GATT meeting that began to consider trade liberalisation in these important New Zealand export products.

Part of the reductions in restrictions on exporters after 1986 was the result of the admission of new members to the WTO. Since 1995 the successor to GATT, the WTO has encouraged new members to adopt freer trade regimes. When China joined the WTO in 2001 it offered to remove more trade restrictions than any earlier entrants to the GATT or the WTO had provided. Vietnam's accession to the WTO (becoming its 150th member) in 2006 involved the relaxation of even more trade restrictions than China had undertaken five years earlier. This did not mean that China and Vietnam removed all their trade restrictions on entry to the WTO, just that they were more forthcoming than earlier new entrants had been.

It is not clear how the trade policies of China and other emerging economies will develop in the future. From 1978 to date China has liberalised its economic policies including its trade policies so that farming is no longer penalised by having to pay input prices that are above world prices. This puts agriculture and manufacturing on a 'level playing field' in that country. In the future China could take this policy a step further. In a worst-case scenario, it could increasingly subsidise its farm sector by pursuing the South Korean model. South Korea taxed its agricultural sector by around 30 per cent in the 1950s but now subsidises the sector at a rate of over 160 per cent (relative to manufacturing) – one of the highest levels of agricultural subsidisation in the world. However, China is more self-sufficient in food products (98 per cent) than South Korea (87 per cent) and, accordingly, the incentive for China to become highly protectionist in the future on mercantilist grounds, like South Korea, is lower.

The current Doha Round of WTO trade negotiations began in 2001 but it has stalled. It had been hoped that a successful outcome to the Doha Round would further reduce trade restrictions on food and agricultural products. It is not known when or if these discussions will be resumed.

Agricultural trade protectionism is difficult for New Zealand to deal with in multilateral trade negotiations (WTO) and especially in bilateral negotiations, because larger economies (with greater influence) want to protect their farm sectors. Global agricultural trade negotiations are caught in what economists call a 'prisoner's dilemma'. If the EU and the US agreed simultaneously to reduce their agricultural protection, their farm sectors would be largely unaffected because world prices would rise to the internal price levels in these economies. However, not knowing if the other player will follow suit, neither will make the first move. It has proven very difficult to resolve this impasse in 63 years of effort.

The Doha WTO Round was initiated at a WTO ministerial conference in Seattle that witnessed perhaps the biggest anti-trade riots ever seen. For this reason, Doha discussions got off to a bad start amidst an atmosphere of political uncertainty. In this environment many countries accelerated their efforts to bypass the multilateral trade framework (WTO) in favour of regional trade agreements.

The first thing to notice about regional trade agreements is the titles of the treaties. They are usually called 'free' trade agreements but it is very rare for the treaties to involve the removal of all trade restrictions between the parties. Indeed, some regional trade agreements like the ASEAN agreement (Southeast Asia), the MERCOSUR agreement ('Southern Cone' countries of South America) and the original New Zealand Australia Free Trade Agreement (NAFTA) contain hardly any significant reductions in trade barriers.

Regional trade agreements are an even more risky strategy globally than going with the WTO system because regional and bilateral trade agreements are more discriminatory than WTO agreements. Larger countries can easily gain the negotiating advantage over smaller countries in face-to-face talks. New Zealand is attempting to reduce this risk by taking a leadership role in international trade fora.

Influenced by the rise of new markets in Asia, New Zealand has pursued bilateral and regional trade agreements with many economies in recent years. They include Singapore, Hong Kong, Brunei, Malaysia, Australia, Chile and Thailand. New Zealand was the first high-income country to conclude a (so-called) bilateral free trade agreement with China. Regional trade agreements are currently being explored with the US, India, Russia, Vietnam, Peru, Japan, South Korea and the Gulf Cooperation Council (Bahrain, Kuwait, Oman, Qatar, Saudi Arabia and the UAE). It remains to be seen how globalisation and the rise of Asia will reshape the politics of trade for New Zealand in the future.

NEW ZEALAND'S COMPARATIVE ADVANTAGES

New Zealand has an edge in certain exports. These have changed over time from kauri logs and wool in its early history to a much broader range of goods today.

New Zealand produces and exports many goods. In 2006, it exported around 2000 types of products, in a universe of around 5000 product groups in the UN trade classification system at the six-digit level of aggregation. This shows that New Zealand firms have overcome size and geographical challenges to export a diverse set of products, although many of them are exported in small quantities. Most of the 2000 products exported are not final goods. This is in line with global trends toward more traded goods being components rather than final products.

Graph 3.3 **New Zealand's comparative advantages, 2006**

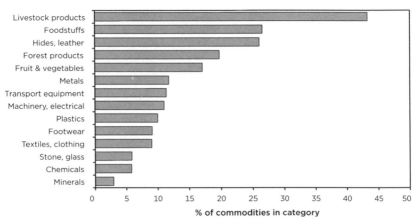

% of commodities in category

Source: Lattimore (2009)

Graph 3.3 summarises the main areas of New Zealand's comparative advantage. For example, New Zealand is very good at exporting livestock products. It is better than the global average in 84 types of livestock products, of 194 possible products (43 per cent shown in chart). New Zealand is also quite good at exporting transport equipment such as luxury boats and electrical machinery such as specialised walkie-talkies. But it isn't very good at exporting chemicals – it has a comparative advantage in only 5 per cent of chemical products.

Comparative advantage refers to an economy's *relative* strength as an exporter – that is, the importance of a particular product in New Zealand's total exports as compared to the importance of that product in the total exports of all other countries. An economy has a revealed comparative advantage in a product when it exports relatively more (of its total exports) than the average of all other countries. New Zealand's highest comparative advantage product is sheepmeats, which comprises a high proportion of its exports. The proportion of sheepmeats in the total exports of all other countries is very low. The ratio is over 50, so New Zealand has a high degree of comparative advantage in this product. New Zealand also has a comparative advantage in certain steel products because the ratio of exports of these products in New Zealand's export mix is higher than the average of all other countries. However, the ratio is only just over 1.0 – the bare minimum required for a revealed comparative advantage.

Of the 2000 products exported by New Zealand in 2006, it had a revealed comparative advantage in 611 of them. New Zealand has at least a few comparative advantages in each of the commodity groupings shown in Graph 3.3. New Zealand food and agricultural products tend to have a higher degree of comparative advantage than other product categories.

New Zealand also exports around 1400 products where it has a comparative *disadvantage* (2000 minus 611). The firms producing these products are internationally *competitive* by virtue of the fact that they have succeeded in marketing them overseas. They tend to be niche products and we can say that New Zealand has a competitive advantage in these 1400 or so goods.

Historically, New Zealand exports were narrower. New Zealand exported wool from the mid-1800s and, with the development of refrigerated shipping in 1882, began exporting dairy products and meat. It developed very strong comparative advantages in these three product areas. In 1914, around 70 per cent of New Zealand exports were meat, wool and dairy products. This proportion rose to around 90 per cent in 1945. Belich (2001) has called this period the 'recolonisation of New Zealand'. This narrowing range of exports was due to the strength of demand for meat, wool and dairy products in the UK and technological change in the New Zealand supply industries.

The import restrictions imposed by New Zealand governments also helped narrow the range of exports by raising the price of protected products on the local market. These import policies encouraged a shift, particularly in manufacturing, of resources towards firms targeting the domestic New Zealand market, with its higher prices. In other words, by protecting New Zealand manufacturers from overseas competition through tariffs and quotas, New Zealand's import substitution policy also reduced the international competitiveness of the non-food manufacturing sector.

Since 1945, the types of New Zealand comparative advantage and sources of export growth have diversified again. In 1965, New Zealand negotiated a limited free trade agreement with Australia called NAFTA; it came into effect on 1 January 1966. This agreement stimulated growth in exports of non-agricultural manufactures, and the share of meat, wool and dairy product exports immediately fell.

The demand for meat and dairy products was reduced in the UK, in part due to that country's entry into the EU in 1973/74. At the same time, New Zealand's import substitution policy has also changed significantly to lower tariffs on imported manufactured goods. In this environment, non-agricultural manufacturing and service industries have become more export competitive. The proportion of New Zealand's total exports in meat, wool and dairy products began to decrease in the 1960s until those products today represent less than 40 per cent of exports.

CONCLUSION

The world economy has become globalised. Asia has become more integrated and integral to global supply chains. Globalisation is still guided by political will, and protectionist policies such as tariffs, taxes and quotas still influence trade. Supra-national agencies such as the WTO are working towards lower trade barriers but consensus is difficult to attain among so many members. Instead, countries like New Zealand are negotiating bilateral and regional trade agreements. However, regional trade agreements are more easily influenced by special interest groups and they do not deliver the potential benefits that a multilateral agreement might.

Despite trade barriers, globalisation has gathered momentum and New Zealand is a part of it. It exports many goods to the world, with significant advantages to the meat, dairy and other land-based industries. New Zealand also exports a number of other products and services, including fashion clothing and specialised transport and electronic equipment. The quantities are often small but the degree of diversity is reasonably wide.

4 Industrial development and policy

INTRODUCTION

The New Zealand economy has changed and will continue to change over time. While the primary sector – which includes agriculture, forestry, fishing and mining – resonates most strongly with the New Zealand image, it accounted for only 7 per cent of the economy in 2006, down from 26 per cent in 1953. The economy is now more heavily weighted towards services. These changes depend on a number of factors, including consumer preferences and technology. Government intervention and policies also shape the direction of the economy, leading to changes in job opportunities, education requirements and choice of places to live.

THE STRUCTURE OF PRODUCTION

The economy is made up of all the firms that produce goods or services that consumers and other firms want to buy. The most common way to categorise firms in New Zealand is the Australian and New Zealand Standard Industrial Classification system (ANZSIC), based on a United Nations standard. This system enables us to compare the size of industries in New Zealand with those in other countries.

Before ANZSIC was implemented, the New Zealand economist A.G.B. Fisher, in the 1920s, aggregated industries into sectors based on the level of processing. The *primary* sector refers to industries that produce raw materials. Agriculture, forestry, mining and fishing are placed in this category. The *secondary* sector (also called the manufacturing or industrial sector) refers to industries that transform raw materials into consumer goods. These are products that are purchased by households or capital goods that are purchased by firms as part of their productive stock of machinery, equipment and infrastructure. The secondary sector develops food, clothing, machinery and equipment, chemicals and a host of other products. The *tertiary* sector (services) refers to producers of intangible goods. It includes banking, real estate, retailing, hospitality, education, health and government.

The size of some key New Zealand industries can be seen in Table 4.1. Services is by far the largest sector of the New Zealand economy (77 per cent), with the manufacturing sector in second place (16 per cent) and the primary sector (farming, forestry, mining and fishing) the smallest (7 per cent). The relative sizes of these sectors changes as the economy develops. More specifically, as real GDP per capita rises, households demand relatively more 'luxury' (discretionary, sophisticated or novel) products and services, and relatively fewer basic (staple) goods and services. This phenomenon is known as Engel's Law. Many of these luxury products are produced by the services sector and this sector tends to grow relative to the other two sectors over time.

There has been a gradual shift in the composition of the economy over time. In 1953 the services sector represented only 52 per cent of GDP (77 per cent in 2006), manufacturing 22 per cent (16 per cent in 2006) and the primary sector 26 per cent (7 per cent in 2006) (Claus et al., 2009). This pattern of sectoral shifts also operates on an international scale through global supply chains. Product innovation and the commercialisation of these innovations (product design, intellectual property registration and production co-ordination) tends to be carried out in high-income countries where the businesses are classified as services industries. The manufacturing processes associated with the product may

Table 4.1 **Abbreviated input–output table, year ending March 2006**

$ millions	Agriculture	Forestry & logging	Mining & quarrying	Food, beverages & tobacco	Wood & wood products	Chemicals, petrol, rubber etc.	Trade, restaurants & hotels
							Inter-industry matrix
Agriculture	1,848	39	0	8,558	1	2	838
Forestry & logging	69	537	1	41	882	3	127
Mining & quarrying	66	1	617	115	12	684	40
Food, beverages & tobacco	271	3	8	2,660	77	108	2,789
Wood & wood products	6	11	0	8	492	5	54
Chemicals, petrol, rubber etc.	905	143	48	598	170	1,146	777
Trade, restaurants & hotels	1,073	124	43	1,157	161	222	3,529
Transport & storage	242	417	119	1,093	210	399	1,749
Finance, insurance etc.	586	89	18	405	94	169	2,927
Other services	821	211	74	1,284	232	553	4,602
Total intermediate inputs	*7,460*	*1,887*	*1,276*	*17,985*	*2,685*	*3,835*	*21,660*
Value added	5,026	913	2,175	6,358	1,287	2,307	19,558
Net (commodity) taxes	460	20	147	1,607	20	1,100	624
Imports	1,094	158	77	1,732	211	3,209	3,111

Source: Claus, Lattimore, Le and Stroombergen (2009).

This input–output table is an abbreviated version of the 21-sector table found on the database for the book (http://sites.google.com/site/eaqubs/). This abbreviated table has the data for ten representative sectors, agriculture (farming) to other services (mainly government services including health and education).

The ten-by-ten matrix in the top-left-hand quadrant is the inter-industry matrix. Each of the ten columns lists the source of all the inputs required by the sector. For example, the agricultural sector used $1,848 million of inputs purchased from within the agricultural sector (inter-firm sales). Agriculture uses $242 million of transport and storage services and $905 million of chemicals (including fertilisers).

There are three rows of primary inputs listed below the sector (inter-industry) matrix after the total intermediate inputs from sectors. The first is value added. This comprises the wages, salaries, profits and rents – the value of labour, capital and land inputs to the sector. Net taxes comprise excise taxes on tobacco, petrol etc., local council rates, any subsidies from governments and, in the case of the finance sector, GST. Imports to the sector are given in the final row.

The total value added for all industries is given in the Total industry column, $135,324 million. This was an estimate of GDP in the year ended March 2006.

On the top right of the table is the demand matrix. It shows the value of consumption by households, government, investment (gross capital formation) and by foreigners (exports). The Food, beverages & tobacco row shows that households consumed $7,864 million of products from this industry. Foreigners consumed $13,384 million via exports.

Transport & storage	Finance, insurance etc.	Other services	Total industry	Demand matrix					
				Household consumption	Government consumption	Gross capital formation	Change stocks	Exports	Final demand
6	25	122	11,678	596	0	23	-2	1,744	2,361
16	2	190	2,073	51	0	37	96	721	905
16	1	96	2,573	95	0	263	0	745	1,103
7	10	209	6,555	7,864	8	41	-171	13,384	21,127
2	5	95	2,838	32	0	30	-26	1,327	1,364
554	29	496	6,662	1,649	97	186	-32	1,889	3,788
935	328	2,186	13,928	20,030	530	3,855	491	6,120	31,026
3,161	98	1,048	9,847	1,640	217	162	3	3,603	5,625
815	6,019	3,919	17,182	7,553	394	1,309	1	698	9,954
1,529	1,879	13,490	29,592	11,940	26,411	1,995	6	3,231	43,581
8,020	9,985	28,346	149,552	70,762	27,677	27,719	460	42,505	169,123
5,548	14,617	40,050	135,324	0	0	0	0	0	0
520	2,091	767	9,822	8,532	671	952	1	785	10,942
1,385	443	4,011	23,977	14,296	312	8,648	235	0	23,492

initially be carried out in a high-income country but then often shift to an emerging economy. The result is that the services sector of the high-income country and the manufacturing sector of the emerging economy grow relatively larger. This has become the standard international product cycle, with Asian economies, and particularly China, prominent in the manufacturing side of these shifts.

The importance of the three sectors in employment parallels their GDP ranking. The services sector is New Zealand's largest employer, followed by manufacturing, followed by the primary sector. However, employment numbers and the characteristics of those employees do not directly follow a sector's GDP contribution. The technology used in different industries varies widely and it influences the characteristics employers seek in their staff. These differences in employee characteristics determine the types of labour markets that exist in New Zealand and the location of those markets.

Industries differ considerably in value added per employee and the amount of capital equipment provided per employee, Table 1.4. For example, the mining and electricity generation sector employs few people but uses a lot of capital and creates a lot of value. By contrast, the retail trade sector employs a lot of people but adds much smaller value per employee. This is because very few employees are required to operate hydro-electric power stations or offshore oil recovery platforms, once constructed. But a retailer needs to employ staff regardless of the initial investment in the building, fit-out and stock.

The number and the qualifications of staff required for each industry also vary. Many capital-heavy industries need highly skilled staff to operate very costly machinery and equipment. For example, the health and education industries require a high proportion of workers with advanced tertiary training, Table 1.4. The forestry industry does not require the same proportion of workers with tertiary training because many of the skills required in forestry work are better transferred to new workers on the job rather than in the classroom.

The size of industries and sectors also varies by region within New Zealand, Table 4.2. The largest employer in the primary sector in 2008 was Auckland, followed by Canterbury and Waikato. The largest employer in manufacturing was also Auckland, followed by Canterbury and Waikato. Auckland is again the largest employer for the services sector, followed by Wellington, Canterbury and Waikato. These locational differences are the subject of a new branch of economics called economic geography. The implications of such differences are explored in the case study by Professor Philip McCann (see p. 151). He examines some of the reasons why Auckland is growing faster than other centres and why this might be linked to globalisation pressures and modern technological advances.

Gender and ethnic balances in employment also vary by industry in New Zealand. This is related to the regional location of industries, the supply of workers with particular skill sets, and the history of formal training, Table 1.4. So, for example, women comprise 57 to 80 per cent of employees in the health, education and textile industries and Maori represent over 30 per cent of employees in the forestry and fishing industries. Given the differences in value added per employee across these industries, these gender and ethnic employment differences have important ramifications for the distribution of income within society.

Table 4.2 **Employment by region and sector, 2008**

	Primary	Intermediate	Tertiary	Total
Northland	9,330	20,560	23,192	53,082
Auckland	42,230	275,580	296,110	613,920
Waikato	28,660	63,780	68,155	160,595
Bay of Plenty	18,030	43,310	44,485	105,825
Gisborne	4,930	5,670	7,529	18,129
Hawke's Bay	13,610	26,300	26,955	66,865
Taranaki	8,740	20,210	17,460	46,410
Manawatu-Wanganui	14,870	36,270	44,700	95,840
Wellington	17,160	74,200	141,970	233,330
Upper North Island	16,250	31,240	26,780	74,270
Canterbury	29,420	112,180	107,780	249,380
Otago	13,140	37,590	41,130	91,860
Southland	8,220	20,090	14,850	43,160
NZ	224,590	767,030	861,130	1,852,750

Source: Statistics NZ
Calculated from LEED data, Infoshare Table reference LED014AA

New Zealand's small domestic market, high wages and distance from foreign markets shape the composition of New Zealand production. The small domestic market is ideal for small- and medium-sized enterprises without large-scale economies. New Zealand is designed for niches. However, the small domestic market size limits the ability of firms to exploit the economies of scale that much of manufacturing technology is designed to enable. Distance from market and the cost of transport mean that New Zealand must be very good at the fields in which it exports. Its firms must focus on scale or high value-added production processes and market niches in order to grow.

The primary sector in New Zealand is comprised of a few industries that have scale economies including forestry, dairy farming, mining, and sheep, beef and wool production. For example, the firms in many New Zealand farming and agricultural processing industries are large by world standards. These primary industries and related manufacturing industries do produce relatively low value-added products, but benefit from scale. This includes timber, gold, coal, crude oil, gas, milk powder, basic cuts of meat and semi-processed wool. The primary sector also produces higher value-added products where scale is less important, including branded wines, highly processed foods and nutriceuticals.

The manufacturing sector (apart from food processing) is focused on the production of niche or short production run goods – for example, healthcare products, replica cars, specialty engineering products, fashion clothing and footwear. These are often components that require highly skilled labour inputs. Other manufactured products may be popular at home but only just being accepted in foreign markets. Often such products have been developed in New Zealand for New Zealand consumers (for example, Weet-Bix). The services sector is driven mainly by domestic requirements and most of its output is sold in New Zealand. The main exceptions to this rule are the tourism and education industries, which export significant quantities of services to foreigners and where New Zealanders import significant amounts of services. There are a number of other services industries that are increasingly tradable internationally. Accounting services, call centres, software production, dental and medical care feature among this emerging group.

ECONOMIC TRENDS

Production systems not only differ between industries but they change over time through technological change. Technological change in a particular industry alters the ratio of inputs to outputs and the ratio of capital to workers required for that industry to remain competitive. It can also alter the skill sets of workers required in a particular industry, and this factor, in turn, alters the relative value of workers with different skill sets and their wage rates – effects that will be discussed in the next chapter.

Over the past 50 years there have been a number of technological advances that may be lumped together under the title of 'office technology'. Office technology consists of a series of developments in firm and office organisation and communications that enables firms to increase their focus on tasks that they are especially good at and outsource tasks that they are less efficient at carrying out. Some examples include moving from a bank of typewriters and typists to computers and getting call centre work done offshore rather than in-house. The result is that production processes for a particular product involve more specialised stages now than they used to and many more firms are involved in the process of transforming raw materials into goods and services. Thus modern supply chains have many more stages or segments than they used to have.

The typical firm now sources raw materials and component parts or services from a large number of input suppliers. Most firms do not produce final goods – that is, products that will be purchased in retail stores. Instead, they produce components, and at the end of the supply chain a select number of firms assemble those components into the final good or service. The inter-firm transactions involved in New Zealand supply chains are illustrated by the connections between industries shown in Table 4.1.

Increased outsourcing and lengthening supply chains are global trends. One result is that most New Zealand exports are not final products but components or raw materials sold to firms overseas that are further along the supply chain. New Zealand's position in this regard (as a high-wage economy) contrasts with that of China (as a low-wage economy), which tends to specialise in the final assembly of products – particularly electrical machinery and equipment. Accordingly, China requires a large number of wooden pallets and crates for its exports but land for trees is scarce. New Zealand has relatively abundant land for trees so it exports logs to China to be transformed into pallets and crates. China also requires large imports of computer chips, integrated circuits (its second-largest import after oil) and software packages to carry out the manufacturing processes that it specialises in. As earlier noted, these components are usually designed in high-income countries, manufactured in other countries and exported to China.

It is worth noting two additional points about supply chains. First, the value that can be added at a certain production stage is not determined by its position along a supply chain. Value added is often greatest towards the beginning of supply chains because at this stage very scarce resources are often required. These might be physical resources such as rare metals only found in select countries or human resources such as design and co-ordination skills. China is the world's largest exporter, but its value added per unit of exports is low because it concentrates on final assembly – a process that can usually be carried out by unskilled workers with on-the-job training.

The second point is that technological changes can have major effects on firms and the workforce in an economy because they alter a country's comparative advantages. The opening up of China after 1978 introduced hundreds of millions of workers to globally integrated labour markets. Many of these workers were skilled at assembly operations. Comparative advantage in assembly shifted from OECD countries to China, while comparative advantages in innovation, design and co-ordination were reinforced in high-income countries. Comparative advantages in China will change again as real wages increase as a result of their high GDP growth rate. Economies such as Vietnam will emerge as competitors.

INVESTMENT

The production of goods and services is a long process that begins with an idea. Sometimes this idea leads to the establishment or expansion of a firm through the financing and purchase of capital goods that will serve as the basis for eventual supply. It takes time to set up a physical plant, and capital goods are often expected to last for years or even decades. It is risky for firms to expand their production capacity because they are forced to make forecasts far into the future. The forecasts are the views of the managers and board members at the time the investment is made. If the general business mood is positive, firms will tend to invest more in capital goods; if it is negative, they will invest less by cancelling or postponing expansion projects.

Graph 4.1 **Investment, quarterly, 1970–2010**

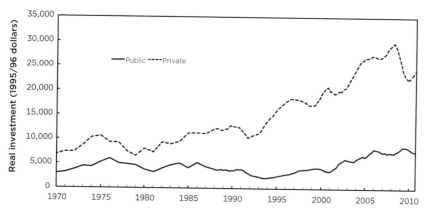

Source: Statistics NZ
Private investment data is sourced from:
    1961–1987: Statistics NZ, Long Term Data Series, Table E.3.2
    1987–current: Statistics NZ, SNCQ.S3RP51T1S
Public investment is calculated by subtracting private investment from total investment, which is sourced from:
    1961–1987: Statistics NZ, Long Term Data Series, Table E.3.2
    1987–current: Statistics NZ, SNCQ.S3RP51T4S

The result of this individual behaviour when spread across all firms is that total private business investment fluctuates from year to year, Graph 4.1. Business opinion is influenced by both the market outlook in New Zealand and the world market outlook as it might affect firm profitability here. From 1992 to mid-2008, private investment trended strongly upwards as compared to the period from 1978 to 1991. This change was the result of the privatisation of a number of government firms during the economic reforms and the creation of an economy more receptive to private investment. Increased investment was also influenced by more liberal lending policies. Private investment is mainly in-house construction, commercial buildings, transport equipment, plant, machinery and equipment, and intangibles such as software and oil exploration.

Private investment over this period did not increase smoothly. In 1997 the Asian Financial Crisis struck and firms expected that the demand for New Zealand exports would fall. Real private investment declined as a result. Between 2001 and 2007, private investment again rose strongly. Then, high interest rates, a domestic recession and the aftermath of the Global Financial Crisis reduced the need for new capacity and the economic outlook became uncertain. As a result, private investment fell sharply from mid-2008.

Changes in economic conditions do not always show up in investment straight away, however, as some investment projects have long lives. For example, an office building may take two years to build and it will generally be completed even if economic conditions change halfway through the construction.

The government also invests in many areas of the economy, but it tends to focus on roads, bridges, schools, hospitals and the like. Investment in these areas tends to be unrelated to the private sector investment cycle. However, the government can increase investment during recessions to try and offset weakness in private sector investment and employment.

Real public investment fell after 1986 as the government reduced spending to improve its financial position. Public investment began to recover from the mid-1990s, Graph 4.1. It rose rapidly again from 2001 to reach a new plateau around 2006. Public investment over the period 2008 to 2010 was boosted by many public sector projects, such as the construction of roads and prisons, being fast-tracked to offset the recession.

ECONOMIC FLUCTUATIONS

As we have just discussed, private investment is sensitive to forecasts of demand – demand for goods by households and by other firms. The product composition of demand is continually changing. Some products are going out of fashion and new products are being produced all the time. Customers are also sensitive to a wide range of factors in deciding how much to buy overall. As a result, there is a fine balance between aggregate supply and aggregate demand and that balance is often disturbed by economic forces and by market sentiment. When aggregate demand falls it automatically induces a fall in aggregate supply and investment in future production plans is reduced. When aggregate demand rises the opposite sequence occurs. Business cycles are created by these processes. These business cycles cause economic fluctuations over and above the continuous technology- and consumer-driven pressures for change in particular markets.

Graph 4.2 **GDP and employment growth, 1970–2010**

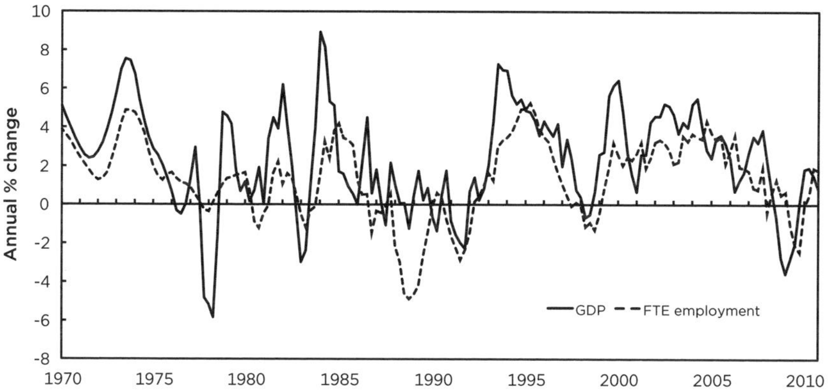

Source: Statistics NZ
GDP data as per Graph 1.1
Full-time equivalent (FTE) employment calculated from:
   1956–1986: Statistics NZ, Long Term Data Series, Table B.1.7, Chappell series
   1986–current: Statistics NZ, full time is HLFQ.S5GS and part time is HLFQ.S5HS

Fluctuations in GDP caused by business cycles and economic shocks are accompanied by changes in employment. As Graph 4.2 shows, employment changes tend to follow changes in GDP. Recruiting and staff training is expensive, so firms usually do not dismiss staff when output first falls in a recession. At the other end of the cycle, firms usually do not re-hire staff as soon as output starts to trend upwards – they wait for confirmation of a recovery. This means that percentage changes in employment tend to be less than and lag behind changes in GDP. So, the economic booms of 1973, 1984, 1993 and those of the 2000s were accompanied by a greater increase in GDP than employment growth. Similarly, the recessions of 1978 and 1983 led to smaller reductions in employment than the fall in GDP.

An exception to this general rule occurred from 1986 to 1990, when the recession induced deep job losses. This was partly caused by government policy. Beginning in 1984, the government's radical economic reforms led to redundancies in government departments and reductions in import restrictions that resulted in a 5 per cent reduction in employment.

PRODUCTIVITY TRENDS

A key macroeconomic indicator is labour productivity – a measure of how much we each produce per unit of effort. The economy will be more productive if it uses more highly skilled labour, better-quality capital and improved technology. A more productive economy will produce more output for the same amount of inputs or resources. Productivity is an important driver of output, value added, incomes and economic efficiency.

Overall labour productivity can be measured by the ratio of GDP to employment (that is, the real value of output per hour worked), Graph 4.3. Between 1970 and 2010 the trend in labour productivity was upwards. However, there was some volatility in the difficult economic times of the 1970s, and over the past decade productivity has not improved. This is reflected in New Zealand's incomes falling relative to our closest neighbour Australia and other peers.

Labour productivity growth in New Zealand has also been uneven across industries. Between 1986 and 2008, productivity growth was strongest in agriculture, electricity, gas and water, transport and storage, and especially in communication services. By contrast, labour productivity has declined in cultural and recreational services, accommodation, cafés and restaurants. Labour productivity growth has been slow in mining and manufacturing. These differences are partly the result of different labour/capital ratios. It is difficult to increase labour productivity in the services sector because businesses like hotels and cafés are, by necessity, labour intensive. However, technological breakthroughs have boosted productivity in sectors such as communications. Technological change can have very positive effects on labour productivity.

Graph 4.3 **Labour productivity, 1970–2010**

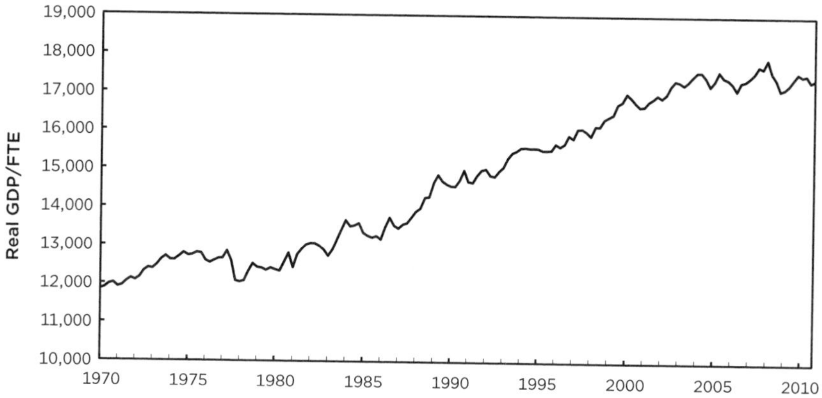

Source: Statistics NZ
Labour productivity is calculated by dividing gross domestic product (Graph 1.1) by full-time equivalent employees (Graph 4.2)

As we have seen, when investment and real GDP rise on the upswing of a business cycle, employment increases often lag and this causes an increase in labour productivity. On the downswing, declines in real GDP growth are usually not accompanied by immediate layoffs so labour productivity falls. You can see these effects in Graph 4.3 in the period around the 2008 recession. Labour productivity growth in New Zealand slowed down in 2007 as GDP growth fell heading into the recession. It increased in 2009 as the economy came out of the recession.

Many people have compared New Zealand with Australia's faster growth in overall labour productivity and higher wages. This concern has led to numerous studies over the past few years, particularly by the Treasury, on why New Zealand's overall labour productivity growth has been lower than in Australia. Various propositions have been advanced but the evidence remains inconclusive.

Graph 4.4 **Measured sector multifactor productivity, annual, 1986–2008**

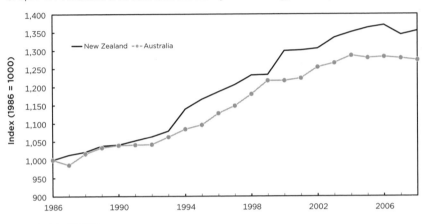

Source: Statistics NZ (2010)

A better measure of productivity change is an index of multifactor productivity for the sectors of the economy where we can be confident that the values used in the index are accurate. This metric is measured sector multifactor productivity, Graph 4.4.

One problem with the overall labour productivity index is that some major industries like the government sector produce outputs that are not traded in markets. We know that the value added in these industries is not correctly measured. A second problem with the labour productivity index is that resource inputs such as capital equipment are excluded from the computation.

The measured sector multifactor productivity index deals with both these issues. It ignores industries where there are not proper market valuations of output and value added and it computes the productivity of both labour and capital inputs. The results obtained by making these corrections are interesting.

THE NEW ZEALAND ECONOMY

Multifactor productivity in New Zealand's measured sector appears to have grown faster than in Australia over the period 1993 to 2006, Graph 4.4. There was a fall in the New Zealand index in 2007 that might be attributable to the recession, but New Zealand's index of measured sector multifactor productivity still remained higher than Australia's. If the measured sector indices prove to be accurate, then the wage gaps with Australia cannot be attributed to poorer multifactor productivity in the measured sectors of the New Zealand economy. We say 'if' because inter-country comparisons of this type assume that the data is fully comparable, which may turn out not to be the case on fuller examination.

New Zealand multifactor productivity between 1986 and 2008 has grown fastest in agriculture, transport and storage, communication services, finance and insurance. Multifactor productivity has gone down in mining, electricity, gas and water, construction, and cultural and recreational services.

PRODUCTION POLICIES

New Zealand government policies also influence production because they change the market incentives for producing certain goods and services. Furthermore, incentives have flow-on effects that alter economic behaviour. Government can be involved directly through the ownership of businesses that are not operated on commercial lines. It can also influence the composition of firms and industries through subsidies, taxes or regulations. These policies may apply directly or indirectly by favouring some industries at the expense of others. That is to say, government can change the balance of industries in the economy. The influences can be quite subtle and the changing balance of industries can be difficult to detect.

For example, when the government provides subsidies for big-budget films in New Zealand, then the firms making big-budget films have higher revenues. Firms making small-budget films do not get higher revenues. Economic efficiency may be affected, depending on what happens as a result of the differential revenues. Firms making big-budget films might get to make more films or might not – perhaps New Zealand gets big-budget films regardless. The presence of the subsidy, however, creates an incentive for valuable resources to flow into big-budget film enterprises and these resources have to come from other firms and industries in the economy because New Zealand has a finite supply of resources. Accordingly, the original balance of firms in the economy may be changed by the subsidy. Government provides a number of subsidies of this type. It currently provides subsidies for export market research, for events and facilities, for example.

A second area of production policy concerns the partial or complete public ownership of particular firms. State-owned enterprises are maintained in electricity reticulation and generation because they control important national assets. Air New Zealand was privatised in 1989; however, the majority of shares in Air New Zealand were purchased back by the government in 2001 when the airline got into financial difficulties. It was viewed as an iconic New Zealand company that could not be allowed to fail.

Taxes are also sometimes used to reduce production in certain sectors or to change how particular products are produced. For example, global concern over climate change has led New Zealand to join international treaties aimed at reducing greenhouse gas emissions. The government has recently introduced carbon taxes on firms producing greenhouse gases that will discourage the expansion of coal-fired power, dairy and cement plants. Conversely, the policy will encourage tree planting by helping to create carbon sink revenues for forest owners.

Other forms of government production policy also have broad effects on economic activity. Three types of production policy are particularly important: competition policy, regulatory policy and trade policy.

Firm competition is monitored in New Zealand by the Commerce Commission. Sometimes firms grow, or merge with other firms, to such a size that they become 'market makers' rather than 'market takers', exerting sufficient dominance that the market becomes inefficient. The firms are virtual monopolists, single sellers (or monopsonists, single buyers). These dominant firms will want to maximise profits by raising prices. Buyers have little alternative but to pay the high price as there is no competition to buy from. This creates a deadweight loss in the economy and is inefficient. The Commerce Commission controls this acquisition of market power by regulating mergers between firms. It can also regulate prices in areas where there is insufficient competition – for example, airports.

Not all economists agree that competition policy should be used to limit the size of expanding firms. Two counter-arguments are made. First, the New Zealand economy is comprised of small markets by world standards, so it is difficult for firms to gain international competitiveness in the face of competition law. Second, while monopolists tend to raise consumer prices and thereby reduce economic welfare, those higher prices attract new firms to innovate and enter the industry. This can create more competition and increase economic welfare over the longer term. The problem might resolve itself.

The New Zealand government sometimes bypasses the Commerce Commission's controls by allowing mergers under special legislation that regulates the behaviour of a firm. When two large dairy co-operatives wanted to merge to form Fonterra in 2000, for example, the government intervened to allow the merger. However, because Fonterra would be a virtual monopsonist – controlling over 90 per cent of raw milk purchases in New Zealand – conditions were imposed. This is an example of regulatory policy instead of competition policy being used to promote competition in markets. Governments also use state ownership as a means of influencing market competition. Kiwibank, for example, was created to increase competition in retail banking.

Regulatory policy is the second broad area of government intervention in production. There has been a resurgence of regulatory policy in New Zealand, and around the world, in recent decades. This resurgence followed a period of regulation after World War II and then a period of deregulation from around 1970 to 1990.

Today, there are regulatory policies setting prices in telecommunications and it is likely that price or profit regulations will be extended to other concentrated industries like gas reticulation. Some of these industries are examples of 'natural monopoly' where economies of scale are so strong that an industry consisting of a single firm will be the lowest-cost arrangement but also the arrangement with the greatest opportunity to charge monopoly prices.

The regulation of prices, other terms of sale or the profits of firms is a difficult area for government intervention. It is not in the interests of society to constrain technological improvements that are the basis for economic development. Furthermore, price and profit regulation requires a great deal of information about participants in the industry. Government officials are not in the best position to discover a firm's true costs, and accounting statistics can change depending on who is asking the question.

The final area of government intervention that shapes production in the economy is trade policy. Historically, New Zealand relied heavily on licences and tariffs on imports to increase incentives for the production of goods that substitute for imports. As discussed in earlier chapters, this import substitution policy has been largely removed over the past 30 years so that restrictions on imports are now similar to those in other high-income countries – except in food and agriculture where New Zealand has lower barriers than most other countries, Table 4.3.

Table 4.3 **New Zealand import restrictions**
Weighted average applied tariffs (%) 2001

	Agriculture & food	Other Primary	Other manufacturing	All tradables
World	16.8	1.2	4.1	4.9
High-income countries	14.1	0.1	1.8	2.5
Developing countries	19.5	3.1	7.3	8.1
New Zealand	2.0	0.0	2.3	2.2

Source: GTAP version 6.2 database, www.gtap.org

The remaining tariff of 2.2 per cent on imports creates a small bias in the production of all internationally tradable goods because it raises the domestic price of imports and increases the incentive to produce import substitutes. Tariffs on imports can hurt exporters in two ways. First, tariffs increase the cost of inputs. As the input–output table (Table 4.1) shows, all industries are dependent on one another. Import substitute industries produce goods using resources that export industries need as inputs. Accordingly, import restrictions raise the cost of producing exports. Second, tariffs crowd out investment in the export sector. Import restrictions encourage investment in import substitute production and discourage investment in export industries. Tariffs are usually economically inefficient in terms of value added and employment.

Historically, the incentive to produce import substitutes, and the consequent disincentive to produce for export, was much stronger than it is today. This is illustrated in Graph 4.5 by the ratio of government assistance to agriculture (the major export sector) versus import protection afforded the import substitute sector.

GRAPH 4.5 **Relative rate of agricultural assistance, 5-yearly, 1955–2005**

Source: Anderson et al. (2007)

From 1955 to 1974 the rate of assistance to agriculture relative to other tradable products varied between minus 16 and minus 24 per cent – meaning that agriculture was effectively taxed by between 16 and 24 per cent. In recent years that export tax has been reduced to single-digit levels.

Another trade policy that assists some firms is anti-dumping duty. These taxes are applied to imports where a local competing firm can convince government that the foreign manufacturer is selling below cost in the New Zealand market. This provision was adopted by the GATT in 1947 as a way of disciplining global monopolists. Before World War II such firms were usually resident in developed countries. Today, anti-dumping duties are more often applied to imports from developing countries. When New Zealand applies such duties they are essentially putting another tariff on imports. The foreign manufacturers are seldom, if ever, global monopolists like Microsoft or Intel. In recent decades New Zealand has applied anti-dumping duties on whiteware goods, shoes, clothing and other selected products. Anti-dumping duties are an example of policy inertia. They are an inefficient and discriminatory policy in today's world (against low-income countries) but are difficult to rescind, having been on the books of the WTO since 1947.

The final type of trade policy intervention concerns government exchange rate manipulation. The New Zealand government has not manipulated the exchange rate to change the production mix of the economy since 1985 when the dollar was fully floated. However, exchange rate manipulation is currently an issue between China and its trading partners so it is included in this policy list.

The Chinese government (and some other Asian governments) does not permit its currency to fully float. Over the past decade or so it has set its exchange rate against the US dollar at a rate where central bank reserves of US dollars have accumulated rapidly and to very high levels (around 2 trillion US dollars). The US and EU governments argue that if China allowed its currency to float it would appreciate against the US dollar and the euro, raising Chinese export prices and dampening the large flow of Chinese exports to the West. The foreign governments see the Chinese exchange rate policy as an implicit export subsidy – a trade policy stimulating exports.

In principle, undervalued exchange rates could be a form of export subsidisation and overvalued exchange rates can be a form of export tax. Indeed, New Zealand used an overvalued exchange rate for just this purpose in the 1970s. However, the Chinese exchange rate policy question is more complex than this simple equation for three reasons. First, it is not clear that the Chinese currency is actually undervalued. Second, emerging economies should be wary of global financial crises as many of them have suffered greatly in recent decades as a result of them. One of the protections against such crises involves foreign exchange reserves. Third, the Chinese government might well question the motives of the US and EU. Both economies are currently reliant on investors holding large and increasing quantities of their governments' bonds to deal with the aftermath of the Global Financial Crisis. China is one of the largest holders of these bonds.

CONCLUSION

The economy is always changing, shaped by changes in consumer preferences, globalisation, technology and productivity. Government intervention and policies influence the mix of industries that make up the economy. For example, the New Zealand economy is now much more services-based than it was in the 1950s when agriculture and manufacturing were more prominent. This has led to changes in the types of jobs, the location of jobs and the skill sets required for employment today. The production structure of the economy determines the types of labour markets within it. This is the subject of the next chapter.

Increases in productivity are crucial to stimulate increases in wages and incomes, and these, in turn, influence consumer preferences. We end up with more city dwellers and a greater concentration of firms providing services such as cafés and restaurants.

5 Labour markets and policy

INTRODUCTION

Employment serves two main functions: it is a mechanism for generating income and it is a means of participating in society. Government policies shape important elements of the labour market – including the nature of bargaining, wage rates, hours of work, qualifications, and health and safety requirements.

The composition and performance of labour markets is described with its own terminology. The total population of the country between the ages of 15 and 64 is termed the 'working-age population'. Over the past 40 years the New Zealand working-age population has steadily increased from around 1.9 million in 1970 to 3.4 million in 2010. The size and composition of the working-age population are driven by population growth and net long-term migration.

The 'labour force' is that part of the working-age population who are in paid work or are prepared to take a job if it is offered to them. The proportion of the working-age population who are in the labour force is called the 'participation rate'. Participation rates vary among social groups. Women, full-time students and retirees in the 15 to 64 age range, for example, all have lower than average participation rates.

Graph 5.1 **Composition of the labour market, September quarter 2010**

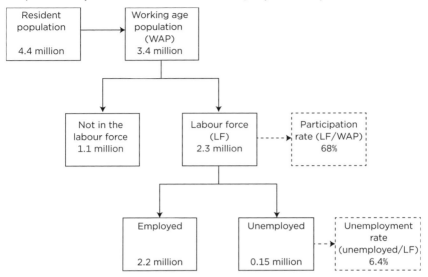

Source: Statistics NZ, Household Labour Force Survey tables

Graph 5.2 **Labour force participation rate, 1970–2010**

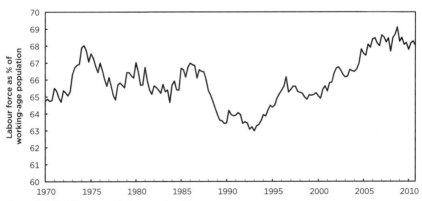

Source: Statistics NZ
1970–1986: Participation rate calculated as the sum of employed and unemployed persons divided by working-age population. Employment from Graph 4.2, unemployment rate from Graph 2.3 and working-age population from Statistics NZ Long Term Data Series, Table B.1.5
1986–current: Statistics NZ, HLFQ.S1E3S

The participation rate of people of working age in the labour force is also quite variable over time, Graph 5.2. When the economy is in recession participation rates often fall. People who have been laid off will sometimes move into full-time training to develop new skills or become despondent about finding a paid job and leave the labour force. In New Zealand the overall participation rate fell during and after the 1985, 1997 and 2008 recessions. Generally, participation rates increase on upswings in the business cycle – for example, from 1993 and 2001.

Labour force participation is also influenced by other factors, including government policy. If wage rates increase for young people or older people, or if tertiary education fees rise, the participation rate will typically rise. If welfare benefits for single parents rise, the participation rate can be expected to fall.

From a historical perspective, the large decline in the participation rate at the time of the 1980s economic reforms (from 67 per cent in 1986 to less than 63 per cent in 1993) indicates the severity of social disruption and resource reallocation. Around 60,000 people exited the labour force. Retention rates at high school increased and enrolments in tertiary training rose rapidly during this period. Many chose early retirement.

EMPLOYMENT

Employment is the result of complex matching between workers and firms. Established firms with particular production, marketing, office and logistical processes want to employ people with the skills required or to employ people with the capacity and motivation to develop those skills through training. Many managers also want to match a new entrant's capabilities with their preferred organisational culture. In other words, firms in particular locations attempt to attract the best staff. But firms also seek out locations where the best potential staff live. New companies or firms changing their technologies gravitate to cities or regions where the required skills are most abundant.

Longer supply chains and increasing specialisation have increased the variety of jobs available. Take house building as an example. Formerly a house was built from a plan created directly or indirectly by an architect and constructed by a builder, with plumbing/drainlaying, wiring and window construction carried out by subcontractors. The builder created most of the value added. Today, house planning is often split between architects, draughtsmen, engineers, resource consent application firms, lighting planners, kitchen designers, interior designers, landscape architects and paint colour specialists. Construction is carried out by builders with assistance from excavation contractors, concrete pumping firms, concrete placers, framing manufacturers, steel portal manufacturers, bricklayers, window and door manufacturers, roofing installers, electricians, plumbers, drainlayers, electronics specialists, solar energy specialists, plasterers, painters, quality control specialists, compliance consent consultants and so on. The builder creates much less of the value added.

Increasing specialisation provides greater job choice for potential employees. More choice makes it harder for young people to find their niche on the first attempt and so employees today change jobs more frequently than in the past. Specialisation also means that some of the skills required by employees are more diverse and are gained on the job. However, there are generic skills (for example, reading, writing and arithmetic) and attitudes (for example, motivation) that employers will look for. University surveys of firms that employ their graduates show managers often have little idea what qualifications their recent hires have – they simply know they have a degree from Waikato or Lincoln University. Wage differentials increase for skilled workers as specialisation grows, but skills take time to acquire. This creates a problem for job market entrants until they have finally decided on the type of job to pursue.

In 2010, 2.2 million people in the labour force were employed and 150,000 people were unemployed, Graph 5.1. The unemployment rate was around 6.4 per cent of the labour force. Most people in the labour force were employed in full-time jobs but the number employed in part-time jobs has been steadily increasing since 1970, Graph 5.3.

Graph 5.3 **Employment, 1970–2010**

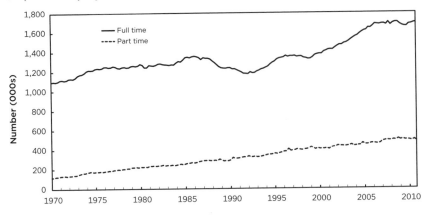

Source: Statistics NZ
As per Graph 4.2

Graph 5.4 **Long-term real wage rates, 1957–2010**

Source: Statistics NZ
1957–1978: Real average hourly earnings including overtime, Statistics NZ, Infoshare Table reference: ERNOO1AA
1978–1992: Prevailing wage rate index, deflated by CPI from Graph 2.2, Statistics NZ, Infoshare Table reference: PWI007AA
1992–current: Labour cost index, deflated by CPI from Graph 2.2, Statistics NZ, EESQ.SASZ9Z

Full-time job availability has been volatile in New Zealand. The number of full-time jobs fell after the 1984 reforms until the restructuring was completed nearly a decade later. Full-time jobs also

THE NEW ZEALAND ECONOMY

fell after the Asian Financial Crisis and more recently following the 2008 recession. Part-time jobs have been less vulnerable to the economic cycle over the past 40 years. They have increased fairly steadily from just over 100,000 in 1970 to almost 500,000 in 2010. Part-time jobs have become more attractive to people who are also involved in other activities like dependent care and tertiary study. Industries with more part-time jobs, like retail and accommodation, have become larger employers.

Real wages were 44 per cent higher in 2010 compared to 50 years earlier, Graph 5.4. This trend increase reflects productivity gains, Graph 4.3. However, there was a large bulge in real wages between 1968 and 1984 where the link between economic fundamentals and wages was severed for a period.

Up until 1967, many wage rates were determined by the Arbitration Court. In 1967 a fall in export prices for wool persuaded the Court that there should be no increase in wages. Labour unions would not accept the decision and the arbitration system essentially broke down. Unions and employers returned to direct bargaining. Real wages began to rise after a brief fall in 1968. Export prices then rose rapidly and the real wage rose with them. When the terms of trade fell in 1974, real wages fell too, but they rose rapidly throughout the rest of the 1970s.

This spectacular rise in real wage rates arose from direct bargaining with employers, as just mentioned, but it involved considerable accommodation by government. This government accommodation of real wage increases took a number of forms. The government doubled real public investment over the period 1970 to 1976, Graph 4.1. It provided much funding to the meat and other industries, ostensibly as export subsidies, but which gave unions associated with these industries a great deal of bargaining power. In short, government created a climate that was very conducive to real wage increases.

The real wage rise from 1970 to its peak in 1980 was the result not of improved economic prospects but rather government efforts to buffer the effects of the two oil shocks by increased government foreign borrowing and associated spending policies. The real wage remained at record, and unsustainable, levels until borrowing limits were reached after the second oil shock in 1979.

In 1981 government was forced to step in to rationalise real wage levels – it had run out of options. It chose to introduce wage, price and interest rate controls across the board. Thereafter, the real wage trended quickly downwards until, in 1984, it was at the same level it had been fifteen years earlier.

The real wage kept falling after 1984 as unemployment rose to record levels in the early 1990s, Graph 2.3. When the economy resumed growth at the end of the reform adjustment period, the unemployment rate began to fall and the real wage started to rise again. Over the past 20 years real wages have gradually improved, reflecting better economic performance. Real wages will typically reflect improvements in labour productivity.

UNEMPLOYMENT

Labour markets in New Zealand are dynamic, with employees leaving old jobs and entering new ones regularly. This labour market mobility is illustrated in Table 5.1. The table shows the numbers of people in various age cohorts entering and leaving jobs over the three-month period, October to December 2008. Bear in mind that 2008 was a year in which there was a recession so the labour market was less buoyant than usual.

In the December quarter of 2008 there were around 137,000 employed 15- to 19-year-olds. There were 44,000 new jobs obtained and 31,000 jobs lost for this age group in that three-month period. The number of 15- to 19-year-olds changing jobs was 28 per cent of the total jobs available. That is, the turnover rate was 28 per cent. As the age of workers increases, the turnover rate decreases, although turnover increases again for people over 64 years of age. Job turnover rates for workers in the middle age cohorts hover between 9 and 19 per cent.

The high job turnover for young people reflects the early stage of their careers and the temporary and part-time nature of much employment. When jobs are lost, people who were recently hired are more likely to be laid off.

Table 5.1 **People entering and leaving jobs, December quarter 2008**

Age cohort	Total jobs	Jobs gained	Jobs lost	Turnover rate
15-19	137,490	44,170	30,840	28
20-24	199,650	49,430	46,230	24
25-29	193,230	36,840	36,130	19
30-34	188,050	28,390	27,340	15
35-39	214,060	27,910	25,890	13
40-44	216,500	25,140	22,930	11
45-49	219,400	22,930	20,920	10
50-54	180,960	17,960	16,320	10
55-59	144,210	13,750	12,520	9
60-64	101,290	9,730	8,960	9
65+	57,880	8,080	7,050	14
All ages	1,852,730	284,320	255,140	15

Source: Statistics NZ
Infoshare Table reference LED022AA

Graph 5.5 **Unemployment by age group, 1970-2010**

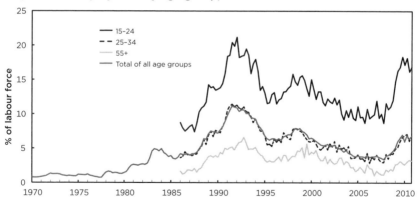

Source: Statistics NZ
Total unemployment rate from Graph 2.3
Unemployment rate by age group calculated from unemployed and
labour force series from Infoshare Table reference: HLF031AA

Unemployment is not spread evenly across the community. For example, the unemployment rate for 15- to 24-year-olds has typically been twice the average rate, Graph 5.5. When the economic reforms of the 1980s were introduced, the unemployment rate for 15- to 24-year-olds rose to over 20 per cent – nearly three times its previous level, Graph 5.5. It has remained at over 10 per cent ever since. Furthermore, the gap between the youth rate and the average rate has widened and it is especially large during recessionary periods – 1991, 1997 and 2008. One of the reasons for this gap is the lower relative availability of unskilled jobs and the demand for increasingly skilled workers. By contrast, the unemployment rates of older workers are much lower than average, though still volatile over the business cycle. Older workers' experience appears to serve them well in the labour market.

Graph 5.6 **Unemployment rate by qualification, 1970–2010**

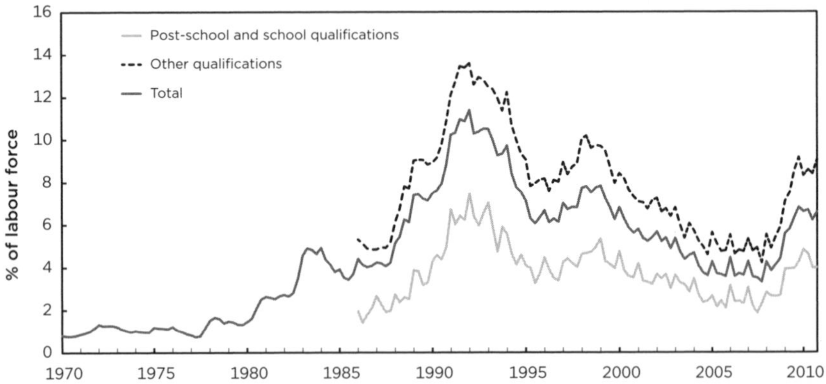

Source: Statistics NZ
Total unemployment rate from Graph 2.3
Unemployment rate by age qualification calculated from unemployed and labour force series from Infoshare Table reference: HLF046AA

Unemployment is unevenly spread on two other measures – qualifications and ethnicity, Graphs 5.6 and 5.7. The first of these graphs illustrates the unemployment rates for people with school and post-school qualifications against those with lower (other) qualifications. The unemployment rate for those with qualifications has been lower since 1985 when the series started. This also partly explains the disparity in unemployment by ethnicity. Maori and Pacific peoples tend to have fewer school and post-school qualifications and hence higher rates of unemployment based on qualifications.

Graph 5.7 **Unemployment rate by ethnicity, December quarter 2009**

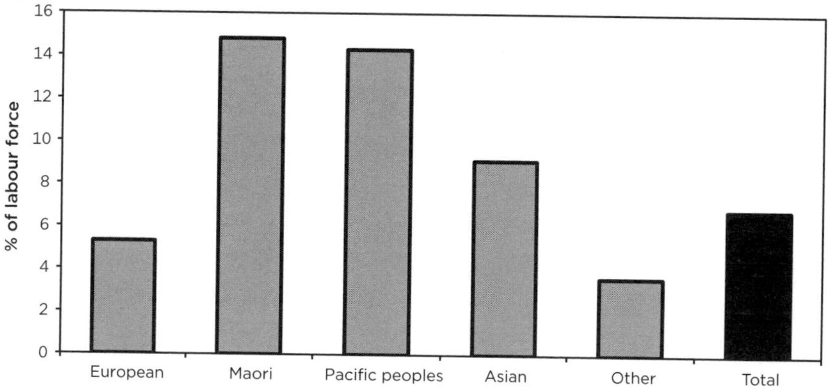

Source: Statistics NZ, Infoshare Table reference: HLF128AA

PRIVATE SECTOR WAGES

Earlier in the chapter we discussed long-term real wage trends for the economy as a whole. Private sector wages are determined by supply and demand changes in labour markets as already outlined. Public sector wages in industries like education, health and core government services are determined through direct negotiation with government which involves somewhat different drivers.

Private sector wages have increased in real terms in recent years, Graph 5.8. They have risen from just under $32,000 per person in 1997 to over $37,000 in 2009, both expressed in 2009 dollar terms. This rise reflects changes in productivity, Graphs 4.3 and 4.4.

The dispersion in wage rates in the private sector has risen since 1997 but only slightly, Graph 5.8. The ratio of decile 10 wages to decile 3 wages has risen from around 2.48 to 2.52. If decile 10 wages reflect margins for highly skilled workers, then they are earning only a marginally larger premium over unskilled counterparts. The slight change in wage dispersion in the private sector implies that globalisation has not seriously disadvantaged lower-paid workers in New Zealand. This phenomenon is consistent with overseas research in other high-income countries. The changing patterns of comparative advantage do change the composition of jobs available in all countries – both low and high income. Jobs are lost in some industries but gained in others and everyone is better off. There are job transition problems, of course, as the labour market processes work their way through, evident in high unemployment in the late 1980s and early 1990s.

Graph 5.8 **Private sector wage movements, 3-yearly, 1997–2009**

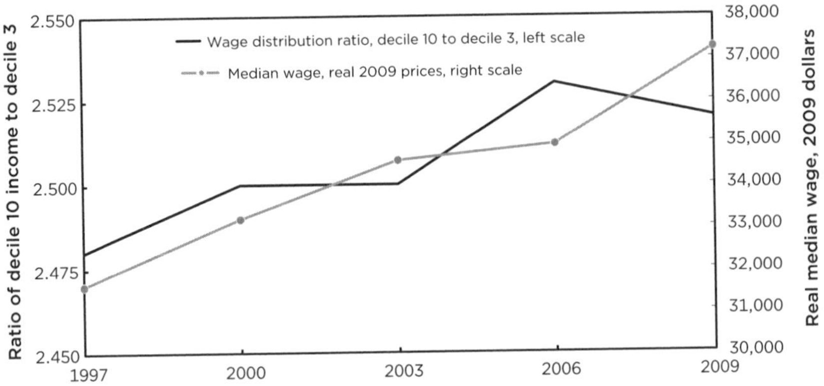

Source: Author's calculations based on data kindly supplied by Statistics NZ
NZ Income Survey, prepared for Ralph Lattimore, job reference number: FIS28856
Note: The graph compares decile 3 and decile 10 because these are mainly full-time employees, while deciles 1 and 2 are mostly part-time.

CONCLUSION

There has been a marked increase in employment in New Zealand since 1970 in line with increases in the population. The number of part-time jobs has risen faster than the number of full-time jobs.

The performance of labour markets in New Zealand over the past 40 years has been quite volatile – both in terms of unemployment and real

THE NEW ZEALAND ECONOMY

wage changes. This volatility mirrors the difficult economic environment of the 1970s and government attempts to buffer the workforce from the full impact of the oil shocks. Once it was realised that New Zealand could not borrow its way out of the difficult times, real wages were reduced through government controls, but this was just the beginning. The 1981 wage controls were immediately followed by the 1984 economic reforms that led to further reductions in real wages as unemployment rose to record levels in the early 1990s.

Over the past 20 years labour markets have been much less volatile with steadier increases in employment. Real wages have also risen in line with increases in labour productivity. The major labour market issue in this recent period is unemployment for youth, Maori and Pacific peoples. The unemployment rates for these groups rose during the reform period and have remained high ever since.

6 International trade and capital flows

INTRODUCTION

International trade and capital flows are very important aspects of the New Zealand economy. Exports account for around a third of GDP; imports represent a similar share. New Zealand exports what it is good at producing, such as dairy and meat, and imports what others are good at, such as TVs and cars. Export and import prices generally respond to global forces and can influence New Zealand's trading patterns. New Zealand saves little in comparison to its investment needs and relies on international capital for funding. So, international capital flows are extremely important.

The balance of payments is a good starting point from which to appreciate the importance of trade and capital flows. On one side is the current account balance. It measures all flows related to imports, exports and profits on investments and businesses. The balancing item is capital flows. If we have a current account deficit, then there will be an equal and opposite capital account surplus, with which the current account 'bill' is settled. Hypothetically, if we bought $3 of imports and sold $2 of exports, then we have spent $1 more than we earned; and this will show as a $1 deficit on our current account. We can pay for this imbalance by reducing enough savings offshore or borrowing enough money from foreigners to put our capital account in credit by $1.

CAPITAL ACCOUNT

The capital account records all international transactions that involve the purchase or sale of assets – money, shares, prized paintings, bonds, land or factories. In recent decades the credits in the New Zealand capital account have outweighed the debits. This surplus in the capital account has mainly been due to New Zealanders (particularly New Zealand banks) borrowing foreign savings to assist in financing business and household investment in plant, equipment and property. There were recent large inflows of foreign savings to finance the housing boom in the decade to 2008.

Investment in New Zealand has tended in recent years to exceed the domestic savings that are available to the local economy. This induces inflows of foreign savings to the economy, producing a surplus in the capital account. This is a good thing, within limits, provided that the economic return is greater than the cost of foreign borrowing. Foreign borrowing increases the net foreign liability position of the economy.

New Zealand's net foreign liability position increased steadily from 75 per cent of GDP in 2004 to 90 per cent of GDP in 2009, Graph 6.1. This period was characterised by rapidly escalating mortgage borrowing. Because there were insufficient domestic savings to fund this expansion, banks brought significant quantities of foreign capital into New Zealand. During the economic recession in 2009 and 2010, growth in both lending and net foreign liabilities slowed. Many commentators and economists worry about New Zealand's large foreign liability position. They argue that if foreign investors were to become more risk averse towards New Zealand and withdrew funds, the economy would suffer via a much lower exchange rate and very high interest rates. Such possibilities put pressure on government to demonstrate sound growth and fiscal planning.

Graph 6.1 **New Zealand net foreign liability position, 1992–2010**

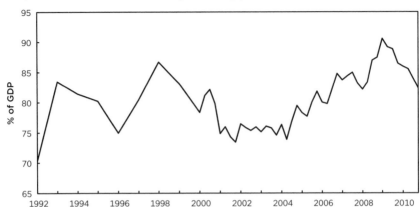

Source: Statistics NZ
1992–2000: Statistics NZ, IIP.S5AAB and SNCA.S1NB01
2000–current: Statistics NZ, BOPQ.S5R13

CURRENT ACCOUNT

This balance of payments subaccount was introduced in Chapter 2. Here we will examine the current account in more detail, especially that part of it that deals with trade in goods. The current account records international transactions associated with exporting and importing goods and services, Table 6.1. This table of the current account is broken up into four sections.

The first section of the current account balance measures trade in things like logs or milk powder – what economists call visible or merchandise goods trade. For the year ending March 2010, visible goods exports were $40.092 billion and visible imports were $37.335 billion – a trade surplus of $2.757 billion. This visible trade balance is usually in surplus on an annual basis for New Zealand.

The second section of the current account balance summarises trade in services. Trade in services comprises tourism and education (classified here as 'transportation', 'travel' or 'other'). The section also includes communication services, computer services and royalties. New Zealand traditionally has a services deficit on transportation because the country is distant from foreign markets and most of the transportation firms that export and import our goods are foreign owned. Historically, travel services were also usually in deficit, because New Zealanders enjoy taking holidays overseas, but in recent years the growth in foreign tourist visits to New Zealand has more than counterbalanced outbound tourism by residents. Overall, the balance on trade in services was a small deficit in 2010 of $219 million.

The third section is the investment income balance. It compares the income earned by New Zealand residents on their foreign investments (credits) with income earned by foreign residents from their investment in New Zealand (debits). This is the return on investment made in the capital account. The balance of income in 2010 was a deficit of $7.627 billion. Readers may want to note that the credits and debits in this part of the current account are classified by the residency of the people rather than their citizenship. For example, the income earned by a foreign resident on their investment in New Zealand could be associated with a New Zealand citizen living in New York or Monaco.

There are small flows in the transfer account, which records aid and other transfer payments. This is the fourth section of Table 6.1.

Overall, the current account was in deficit in 2010 by $4.457 billion.

TRADE ACCOUNT

The first section of the current account in Table 6.1 is called the trade account. The trade account can be broken down very finely into trade by commodity and trade by trading partner. This disaggregation of the trade account is the subject of this part of the chapter.

The importance of exports differs markedly among economies. In China, for example, exports have very low value added. China tends to import components and assemble them into final goods, producing value added for China of only about 10 per cent of the total value of export products.

In New Zealand, by contrast, export value added is very high – 74 per cent in 2006, Graph 6.2. The data in this graph shows the two

Table 6.1 **Current account, year ending March 2010**

	$m
Balance on goods trade	2,757
Exports or trade credits	*40,092*
Imports or trade debits	*37,335*
Balance on services trade	-219
Exports or trade credits	*11,888*
Transportation	2,282
Travel	6,906
Communication	272
Computer & information	324
Royalties & licence fees	242
Other	1,862
Imports or trade debits	*12,107*
Transportation	3,438
Travel	3,994
Communication	308
Computer & information	451
Royalties & licence fees	151
Other	3,765
Balance on income	-7,627
Income from New Zealand investment abroad	*2,285*
Direct investment income	502
Portfolio investment income	1,509
Other investment income	274
Income from foreign investment in New Zealand	*9,912*
Direct investment income	4,922
Portfolio investment income	2,913
Other investment income	2,077
Balance on current transfers	633
Inflow of current transfers	*2,003*
Outflow of current transfers	*1,370*
Current account balance	-4,457

Source: Statistics NZ, Balance of Payments data tables accompanying release

THE NEW ZEALAND ECONOMY

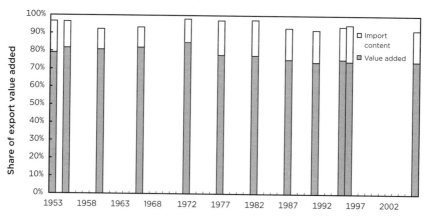

Source: Claus, Lattimore, Le and Stroombergen (2009)

major components of New Zealand exports: value added and the import
content. The small remainder that is not shown explicitly in the graph is
comprised of net New Zealand taxes affecting exports. This high value-
added share means that exports are key drivers of the New Zealand
economy, shaping natural resource use, wages and salaries, and profits to
New Zealand firms. In New Zealand, incomes are much more dependent
on exports than they are in China.

The value-added content of exports is lower in New Zealand than
it was in the 1950s and 1960s. As New Zealand import barriers were
reduced it became more profitable for export firms to import components
in manufacturing. The import content rose from 11 per cent in the 1960s
to 20 per cent in 1996 and fell to 17 per cent in 2006. Interestingly,
import content was also high for a period in the 1950s when government
briefly liberalised imports; only to reimpose blanket import licensing
following a major fall in dairy export prices in 1957.

Taxation on exports has also changed over time. Net taxes plus value
added and import content make up the export value total. In 2006 net
taxes represented 9 per cent of the value of exports – the highest they
have ever been over the period since 1953.

Because trade in visible or merchandise goods used to dominate the economy, we have more timely data on exports and imports of items than we do for the other elements of the current account. However, because it excludes services, the trade account by itself is much less useful today.

Graph 6.3 **Top 10 imports, year ending March 2010**

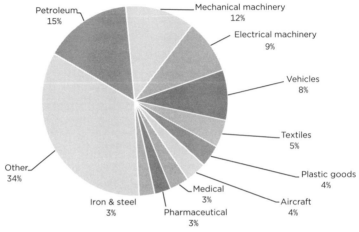

Source: Statistics NZ
Table 6, Overseas Merchandise Trade tables accompanying the Hot Off The Press release

Graphs 6.3 and 6.4 show the top ten New Zealand imports and exports for 2009/10 in data drawn from the trade account. New Zealand has long relied heavily on imported petroleum products and they currently represent 15 per cent of total imports of merchandise goods. Imports are also focused on finished goods not made in New Zealand, such as mechanical machinery (12 per cent), electrical machinery (9 per cent) and vehicles (8 per cent). Imports also include a range of products for further manufacture in New Zealand – textiles (5 per cent), plastics (4 per cent), and iron and steel (3 per cent).

Dairy products are the largest component of visible exports, representing 23 per cent of the total for 2009/10, Graph 6.4. Meat is also very important at 13 per cent. Wool exports are too small to warrant their own category in the graph. The ordering of these and other land-based exports changes a great deal over time. In 1950 the export market shares of wool, meat and dairy products were 41, 16 and 30 per cent respectively. In 1986 they were 12, 16 and 13 per cent.

Graph 6.4 **Top 10 exports, year ending March 2010**

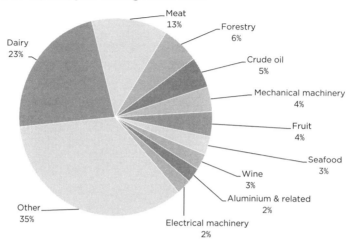

Source: Statistics NZ
Table 5, Overseas Merchandise Trade tables accompanying the Hot Off The Press release

Forestry represents 6 per cent of exports for 2009/10 and crude oil 5 per cent, the latter as a result of successful drilling for petroleum products in recent decades. Aluminium products (2 per cent) are an important export based on the availability of cheap hydro power. The alumina ore used in the production of aluminium is all imported.

Mechanical machinery and electrical machinery are significant exports as well as major imports. Exports of these products provides an interesting example of New Zealand focusing on niche export products with shorter production runs while importing 'commodity' machinery items requiring long production runs.

Fruit represents 4 per cent of merchandise exports and like the pastoral products its composition has changed over time – between apples and kiwifruit, for example. Wine exports have grown rapidly in recent years and now represent 3 per cent of merchandise exports.

Finally, note that the 'other' category in Graph 6.4 is very large at 35 per cent. This reflects the diversity of New Zealand exports discussed in Chapter 3.

Graphs 6.5 and 6.6 outline the geography of New Zealand merchandise exports and imports. Care is required in interpreting these graphs since many traded products are intermediate goods and the bilateral trade is often just one step in what can be a long global supply chain. This is true not only for electronic products and machinery but also for food and agricultural products. For example, many dairy products are exported for use in the manufacture of prepared foods and industrial products by New Zealand's trading partners. Those goods are then often exported to third countries. A further complication results from the global spread of multinational firms. A New Zealand import from South Korea, for example, may be the product of a South Korean firm, or a German firm in South Korea, or a South Korean firm that is contracted to produce a good by a German firm.

Graph 6.5 **Major import sources, year ending March 2010**

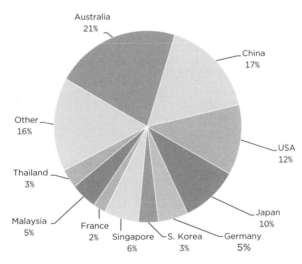

Source: Statistics NZ
Table 4, Overseas Merchandise Trade tables accompanying the Hot Off The Press release

THE NEW ZEALAND ECONOMY

With these caveats in mind, Australia is the most important source of New Zealand imports and this trade has been stimulated by its close proximity, the trade liberalisation programmes adopted by both countries, and the Australia New Zealand Closer Economic Relations Trade Agreement (ANZCERTA) signed in 1983. The next most important import sources are China, the US, Japan, Singapore, Germany and Malaysia. Over 40 per cent of New Zealand merchandise imports originate in Asia. Not surprisingly, the greatest change in recent years has been in imports from China.

Australia is also our major export destination, followed by China, the US, Japan, the UK and South Korea, Graph 6.6. Of the top ten itemised destinations in the graph, 29 per cent of merchandise exports are to Asian countries. Including non-itemised smaller countries, over 40 per cent of all exports go to Asia. Asian countries are New Zealand's fastest-growing export destinations.

Graph 6.6 **Major export destinations, year ending March 2010**

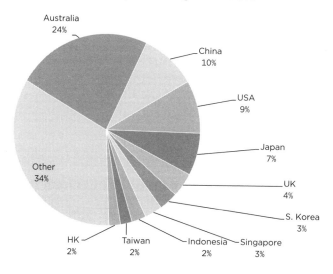

Australia 24%
China 10%
USA 9%
Japan 7%
UK 4%
S. Korea 3%
Singapore 3%
Indonesia 2%
Taiwan 2%
HK 2%
Other 34%

Source: Statistics NZ
Table 3, Overseas Merchandise Trade tables accompanying the Hot Off The Press release

The Asia-Pacific region has the fastest rate of trade growth in the world and is consequently the region of greatest opportunity. Asia also has some of the highest barriers to trade so it is potentially very fruitful ground for diplomatic efforts to reform trade policies.

TRADE AND THE INPUT–OUTPUT TABLE

The nature of New Zealand exports and imports can be examined in more detail in the input–output table, Table 4.1, because it links exports and imports of goods and services to particular industries. That is to say, the input–output figures provide more information on trade in services as well as additional information on trade in merchandise goods.

In 2005/06 the total exports of goods and services, shown in the second-to-last column of Table 4.1, were $42.5 billion. The food, beverage and tobacco industry produced the most export dollars, $13.4 billion, with the agricultural sector exporting another $1.7 billion worth of mostly sheep, beef and dairy products. Food and agricultural products make up 36 per cent of New Zealand's exports of goods and services, which is high for a developed country. It is a statistic that has been discussed widely in New Zealand. Engel's Law suggests that as incomes rise, a smaller proportion of total income is spent on food. That means that food and agricultural products tend to have small elasticities of demand and so some economists predict limited international market growth for these products.

However, while overall growth of world trade in food and agricultural products is relatively slow, the consumption of food and agricultural products that New Zealand produces has risen rapidly in emerging economies such as those of India and China. The income elasticities of demand for meat and dairy products in emerging and developing economies are high compared to developed markets like Japan, the US and the EU. Indeed, New Zealand's fast-growing exports of these products to Asian countries has helped keep its economy more buoyant than comparable economies throughout the Global Financial Crisis. Furthermore, the fastest-growing global export markets within the food, beverages and tobacco grouping are higher-valued products such as wine, honey and prepared foods, and not traditional, lower value-added meat and dairy products.

After food, the next largest export groups are services from the trade, restaurants and hotel industry, $6.1 billion, and transport and storage services, $3.6 billion. These two groups include tourism exports, which have grown rapidly in recent years. Other services produced $3.2 billion in exports in 2005/06. This grouping includes exports of education services, which have also grown rapidly over the past 20 years.

The value of imports in 2005/06 is given in the last row of Table 4.1. Imported inputs to each industry are shown in the industry columns. These imports, totalling $23.9 billion, are heavily concentrated in raw materials like oil and phosphate rock, and in machinery and equipment. The second group of imports are final goods and their values are listed under the categories of consumption by households and government. Total imports of this second group totalled $23.5 billion – so, overall, total imports of goods and services were $47.5 billion in 2005/06.

The input–output table can also be used to measure other features of New Zealand's trading patterns. First, New Zealand's degree of self-sufficiency in particular products can be assessed by comparing the exports of an industry with production used for domestic consumption. For example, exports of food, beverages and tobacco represent 64 per cent of final demand, whereas exports of finance and insurance services only represent 7 per cent of final demand. Second, the export/import balance of each industry can be assessed from the respective row and column. The chemical industry, for example, imported products worth $3.2 billion and exported products worth $1.9 billion in 2005/06.

INTERNATIONAL PRICES

New Zealand's trade patterns are also influenced by changes in import and export prices. When import prices rise, New Zealand must export more or borrow more to maintain imports. When export prices rise, New Zealand can afford to import more.

Import prices are mainly influenced by oil price volatility and a longer-term downward trend in manufactured products tied to globalisation and the rise of Asia. Export prices are mainly influenced by movements in agriculture commodity prices, New Zealand's main exports. These are influenced by weather patterns, global supply and demand, and foreign policy settings.

New Zealand's import price volatility has historically been tied to oil prices, as discussed in Chapter 1. However, New Zealand is now both an exporter and an importer of petroleum products and oil price shocks impact less on the trade accounts than in the past.

Graph 6.7 **Real Korean electrical machinery export prices, SDR index, 1980–2010**

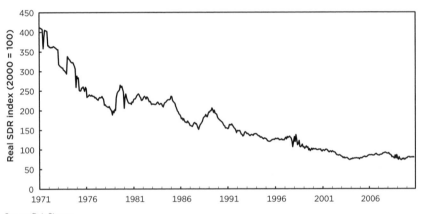

Source: DataStream
Korean capital import price index, DataStream, KOMPIGKPF, converted to USD terms, deflated by US CPI, converted to SDR terms

A declining trend in global manufactured product prices has also been a dominant feature. The real Korean export price index of electrical machinery goods illustrates this downward trend, Graph 6.7. The supply chains for electronics equipment and machinery are very long and involve firms from high-, medium- and low-income countries. Asian countries are prominent in manufacturing, with China carrying out much of the final assembly.

Two trends are important. First, manufactured product prices are less volatile than commodity prices. This is because manufacturing processes can be altered very quickly to match market conditions. In the industries producing machinery and equipment, employment changes tend to act as the buffer for demand changes (rather than farm profitability as in the agricultural commodity case). Second, prices trend downward over the long term. While demand for these products has grown steadily over time, this downward trend in prices is due to rapid technological change in manufacturing processes coupled with the transfer of this technology to lower-wage emerging economies. The trend is a graphic illustration of the effects of globalisation in action.

Graph 6.8 **Real New Zealand farm price of milk, SDR index, 1955–2009**

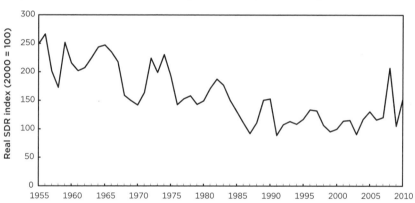

Source: Authors' calculations based on financial statements of the New Zealand Dairy Board, Wellington, 1985, and Ministry of Agriculture and Forestry, Wellington

Another major driver of the terms of trade is dairy prices. Dairy product prices are volatile over time due to global supply shocks such as animal feed price increases, droughts and unexpected dairy policy changes in larger economies like the EU and the US. These shocks can cause price spikes until world demand or supply adjusts.

World dairy product prices over time at the farm gate level are illustrated in Graph 6.8. Over the period from 1955 to around 1990, the real milk price trended downwards. There does not appear to be a strong trend from 1990 to date. The milk price has been quite volatile over the whole period and the spike in 2008 is yet another example of commodity price volatility.

Long-term trends in the milk price are determined by world demand and supply. Population growth and increases in consumer incomes have increased demand, but at the same time improvements in dairy production technology has driven down the cost of milk production worldwide. One rough indicator of the extent of this productivity change since 1955 is the average size of milking herds in New Zealand. In the mid-1950s the average milking herd was around 60 cows, while it is over 500 cows today in the South Island (which is our fastest-growing dairy region). Accordingly, while the world milk price is only 40 per cent of the 1955 level, dairy farmer incomes in real terms have remained stable through productivity gains. Remember that the agricultural sector has one of the fastest rates of productivity change in New Zealand (Chapter 4). In the long run, the most important driver of farm income is productivity change.

CONCLUSION

The New Zealand economy is inextricably connected to the world via trade and capital flows. These connections have deepened and broadened over time. New Zealand exports mainly agricultural goods to the world, while importing oil, industry inputs, cars, electronics and other finished goods.

New Zealand has benefited from a downward trend in global manufactured product prices – a result of globalisation and productivity improvements. Export commodity prices are volatile, but productivity gains and growing demand from emerging markets should continue to underpin New Zealand's export earnings.

7 Capital markets and monetary policy

INTRODUCTION

This chapter focuses on capital markets, which bring together savers and investors in the economy. It is also a useful place to discuss New Zealand monetary policy because it operates through money markets that are closely linked to other capital markets and to savings and investment behaviour. Investment in human and physical capital is a major driver of economic growth.

Capital markets include markets for shares, debt and property. They bring together savers and borrowers; the sellers and buyers in these markets. Monetary policy tries to maintain price stability by influencing the price and quantity of money in the economy by targeting interest rates which affects the incentive to save and invest.

From a real economy point of view (as opposed to a financial view) the process of investment involves giving up the consumption of consumer goods and services, like extra pizzas or hairdos, and investing instead in skilled employees or new machine tools. Investment is critical to economic growth. Businesses and households either need to rely on their own savings or borrow the savings of others to fund investment. The finance sector provides the markets to accomplish this objective.

The share and property markets facilitate investment in firms and property.

This chapter pays special attention to a number of features of these markets that are of current interest in New Zealand – in particular, failures in capital markets, inflation and the role of the Reserve Bank of New Zealand.

CAPITAL MARKETS

Capital markets can be subdivided into three types: equity or share markets; debt or bond markets; and property markets.

Table 7.1 provides estimates of the values of assets in New Zealand, comparing business and housing assets with the size of major financial markets, such as shares, debt and government borrowing. The table illustrates how large capital markets are, relative to national income (or GDP). Official and consistently up-to-date data is not available on total assets and liabilities in the economy, so the data presented should be viewed as illustrative only.

In the sharemarket, a saver can buy shares in a legal entity called a joint stock company that is managed by directors on behalf of all shareholders. The saver then receives dividends paid out of the profits of the company and any capital gain in the market value of the shares. Investment risks are taken on by shareholders. The largest firms listed on the New Zealand sharemarket include Telecom, Fletcher Building, Westpac, The Warehouse and Contact Energy. Anyone is at liberty to buy shares in companies listed on the sharemarket.

Sharemarkets provide both a primary market for the sale of new shares and a secondary market where existing shares may be traded. This allows investors to adjust their portfolio of shares at any time, with the aim of changing the risk profile. The sharemarket is liquid: it doesn't usually take much time to find a buyer for your shares or a seller of shares you want to buy.

Table 7.1 **Illustrative financial and capital metrics, 2008**

	Value ($m)	% of GDP
Key financial indicators[1]		
Money supply		
Cash in circulation	3,525	2%
Broad money (M3 excl. repos)	209,454	114%
Government bonds	31,627	17%
NZ stock market capitalisation	31,323	17.0%
Top 50	31,110	16.9%
Alternative index	213	0.1%
Net asset value of key sectors[2]		
Approximate farm value[3]	231,617	126%
Fonterra[4]	*4,269*	*2%*
Non-rural businesses[5]	601,028	326%
Household wealth[6]		
Value of homes	568,000	309%
Net financial wealth	19,000	10%
Net wealth	587,000	319%
Key debt indicators[7]		
Total debt	298,783	162%
Farm debt	43,446	24%
Business debt	81,014	44%
Household debt	174,323	95%
Housing	161,584	88%
Credit cards	5,122	3%
Other consumer debt	7,617	4%

Source: NZX, QVNZ, RBNZ, MAF, Fonterra, Statistics NZ
Notes:
(1) Values for the end of 2008. Money supply data is sourced from the RBNZ. Government bonds is the amount outstanding at that period. Stock market capitalisation data is sourced from the New Zealand Stock Exchange.
(2) Net asset value is calculated by subtracting total liabilities from total assets. This residual value is attributable to the business owner. Consistent asset and liability data is not available for the business sector in New Zealand.
(3) Farm value is approximate. We used Ministry of Agriculture and Forestry (MAF) data on total land area and multiplied it by average land area value from QVNZ data. We then applied the total asset to land asset ratio in MAF estimates of 'model' farms to estimate total assets. We then subtracted bank debt from total assets to arrive at net asset value. Because this analysis does not take into account detailed assets and liabilities, this value is only a rough approximation.
(4) Fonterra's net asset value is sourced from its annual report.
(5) Non-rural business data is sourced from Statistics NZ's Annual Enterprise Survey.
(6) Household asset and liability estimates are published by the RBNZ.
(7) Debt indicators are published by the RBNZ.

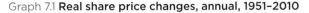

Graph 7.1 **Real share price changes, annual, 1951–2010**

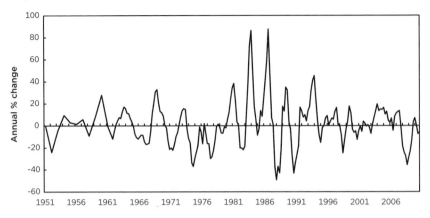

Source: RBNZ, DataStream, Statistics NZ
1950–1988: Reddell and Sleeman (2008)
1988–current: DataStream, TOTMKNZ, deflated by CPI from Graph 2.2

Sharemarket returns have to be reasonably high relative to other investments because shareholders accept business risks in the companies they are buying into. Investors will typically buy a selection of stocks and bonds to balance the risk that some of the investments may not perform. Share prices are quite variable, going through periods of exuberance ('bull markets') and despondency ('bear markets').

Graph 7.1 shows the rapid run-up in share prices in the mid-1980s followed by the 1987 sharemarket crash. The 2008 crash in share prices triggered by the Global Financial Crisis (GFC) is also clear. The New Zealand sharemarket is small relative to other countries, with relatively few listings in important sectors of the economy like agriculture and infrastructure. One probable cause of this feature is New Zealanders' enthusiasm for the property market, discussed below.

A variant on direct investment in the sharemarket is the co-operative. This arrangement is popular in the agricultural sector in New Zealand, with Fonterra the leading example. In a co-operative, a saver has to be a member of the co-operative in order to buy shares. In the case of Fonterra, only milk producers who supply milk to Fonterra can be members – indeed, all suppliers are obliged to buy shares in the co-operative.

THE NEW ZEALAND ECONOMY

Another example of direct investment is the debt or bond market. By buying bonds, a saver is making a loan to a company in return for certain interest payments. Private companies like Contact Energy, Westpac and finance companies, as well as central government, city councils and SOEs such as Transpower and Kiwibank, regularly borrow savings in this way. These enterprises are taking on debt rather than granting an equity share in the enterprise. Because bonds will need to be redeemed in the future, the issuing firm is accepting more risk by selling bonds than they would by selling shares. There are still risks being taken on by bond holders as the risk of company default is borne by the holder, but bond holders are earlier in line than equity holders in the case of default. Bonds can also be bought and sold in secondary markets like shares. In New Zealand, the bond market is relatively small as many businesses borrow funds from banks rather than directly from savers.

Graph 7.2 **Real 90-day bank bill yields, 1990–2010**

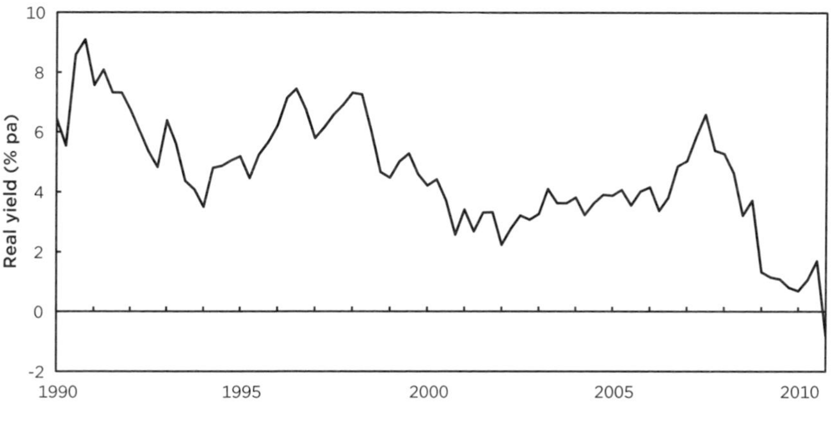

Source: RBNZ, Statistics NZ
90-day bank bill yield: RBNZ, Table B2
Real calculated using inflation from Graph 2.2, using the formula:
r=(1+n)/(1+i)-1
where r is real interest rate, n is nominal interest rate and i is CPI inflation

Real bond yields are cyclical. These cycles reflect changes in the Official Cash Rate (OCR) set by the Reserve Bank and by perceptions of risk

– that is, the ability of businesses to repay debt. So, when economic conditions deteriorate, investors demand premiums over the OCR to compensate them for taking the risk of capital loss. This is illustrated in Graph 7.2 by the rise in bond yields from the mid-2000s as the perceived riskiness of bonds increased. The rapid fall in bond yields from 2007 mirrors the interest rate reductions by the Reserve Bank in the wake of the emerging recession in New Zealand. However, despite a very low OCR, bond yields rose rapidly in 2010 for finance companies that were having solvency problems. Investors demanded a larger interest premium to compensate them for the additional risk.

Property markets are the third type of capital market. They include markets for residential sections, houses, lifestyle blocks, forestry blocks, commercial buildings and farms. Property assets are popular among New Zealand investors. For example, the value of housing accounts for most household wealth, while financial wealth comprises only a small segment.

Graph 7.3 **Real house price inflation and house price to income ratio, 1924–2010**

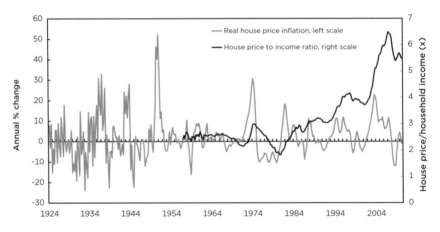

Source: RBNZ, QVNZ, Statistics NZ
1923–1962: Reddell and Sleeman (2008)
1962–current: QVNZ house price data, sourced from RBNZ Key Graph, 'House prices and value of housing stock', deflated by CPI from Graph 2.2
House price to income ratio: Real house price series divided by the real wage index in Graph 5.4 indexed to disposable income to median price ratio as at December 2009 quarter

THE NEW ZEALAND ECONOMY

Real property prices in New Zealand are volatile, Graph 7.3. Real house prices rose sharply after World War II in the face of shortages of building materials but more particularly after government price controls on houses were removed. A sharp fall in real house prices is evident in the late 1950s when the terms of trade fell. The sharp rise in the terms of trade in the early 1970s had the opposite effect.

House price cycles reflect changing conditions in employment, income, net migration, interest rates and regulatory settings. Over the 30 years to 1980, real house prices rose by a modest 2.2 per cent per annum. However, since 1980, house prices have risen more rapidly with increases averaging 5.2 per cent per annum over the 30 years to 2010. This may have been due to a number of factors, including rising real incomes, easier access to mortgages, increasing numbers of relatively wealthy 'baby boomers' buying larger homes, structurally lower interest rates and increasing house construction costs. House prices were 5.7 times the average annual household income in 2009, compared to between 2 and 3 times annual income over the period from 1954 to 1990, Graph 7.3.

There are conflicting views on the long-term outlook for house prices. Some believe house prices need to fall substantially to restore housing affordability while others think house prices will remain higher (relative to incomes) because house demand and supply parameters have changed in fundamental ways. Two factors are of particular interest. The cost of sections for housing has risen over time and productivity in the construction sector has been falling (Chapter 4) – both, perhaps, as a result of central and local government regulations.

FINANCIAL INTERMEDIATION

Financial intermediaries are the 'middlemen' who match up savers and borrowers. Financial intermediation is the process of changing one set of assets and liabilities into another set of assets and liabilities. It is important to understand this intermediation process because capital markets can break down as a result of market failure and government failure. The GFC is a good example of these two types of failure. Some capital markets in the US and in Europe froze for short periods in 2008 and 2009 partly as a result of inadequate government regulations. The crises associated with finance companies in New Zealand in 2007 and 2008 might turn out to be a similar occurrence of these joint failures.

Financial intermediaries can bring together a large pool of savers and borrowers. This enables them to offer investment terms and conditions that suit both parties – conditions that would be difficult for individual investors to create. It is costly for savers to search out borrowers, make sure they are creditworthy and ensure that the debt is repaid on time. A financial institution has scale on its side to manage these issues.

Financial intermediaries include trading banks, insurance companies, investment banks, credit unions, venture capital firms and finance companies. The operations of these firms involve trading bonds and money among themselves in wholesale markets as well as trading in retail markets with savers and investors.

The most important financial intermediaries are the registered trading banks that take retail deposits from savers. Banks provide a payment and financial settlement function for the economy, enabling savers to store deposits and buyers to pay bills to firms for goods or services.

The accumulation of bank deposits gives rise to a variety of interlinked money markets. Banks on-lend most of the deposits accepted from savers to investors wanting to buy houses or new equipment, or else to other banks who have greater lending opportunities. The borrowers pay interest on these funds and that interest pays the cost of operating the bank (including dividends to shareholders) with the residue paid to deposit holders who have savings accounts or term deposits. This is why the cost of the borrowing tends to be higher than the interest rate on deposits.

The financial intermediation sector has undergone significant technical change in recent decades. The global financial industry has developed a large number of products including hedge funds, commodity futures and mortgage-backed securities. New markets have developed around those products. Some of the products are complex in the sense that it is difficult for the purchaser to know how much risk is being taken on. Many of the most complex ones developed overseas are not used in New Zealand and so the economy escaped many of the problems associated with the GFC.

The balance sheet of a typical registered bank looks something like Table 7.2. Consider first the assets on the left-hand side of the balance sheet. 'Settlement cash' refers to the balance of a special account held by the bank at the Reserve Bank to settle its net obligations to other members of the financial system (these obligations occur every day as a result of transactions among customers of the different institutions). The Reserve Bank does not allow a settlement account to move into overdraft, so each financial institution must make sure it has sufficient settlement cash to meet its obligations at the end of each day's trade.

Table 7.2 **Balance sheet for a typical financial institution**

Assets	$m	Liabilities	$m
Settlement cash	2	Deposits & borrowings	
Till cash	3	NZ residents	450
Government bonds	145	Non-residents	300
Loans to customers	730	Reserves & other liabilities	70
Buildings & other assets	120	Shareholders' funds	180
Total assets	1,000	Total liabilities	1,000

'Till cash' is the currency held by an institution to finance the day-to-day deposits and withdrawals of customers. Other liquid assets such as government bonds are also kept in reserve. These can easily be turned into cash if for any reason there is a sudden increase in the level of withdrawals by depositors. The largest asset of a typical bank is its portfolio of 'loans to customers'. The interest on these loans is the principal income source for interest paid on term deposits and dividends paid to bank shareholders.

On the liabilities side, the largest item is the 'deposits and borrowings'. In April 2010 around 40 per cent of these deposits and borrowings by registered banks in New Zealand were from non-residents.

Non-resident 'deposits and borrowings' reveals the dependence of the New Zealand economy on foreign savings (from the proverbial

Japanese housewives and Belgium dentists!). These borrowings are often short term. New Zealand financial institutions must pay what is called a country risk premium for these funds because New Zealand is a small financial market by world standards and foreign brokers are not as familiar with lending risks here as they are in larger countries, Graph 7.4.

Graph 7.4 **New Zealand country risk premium, 1992–2010**

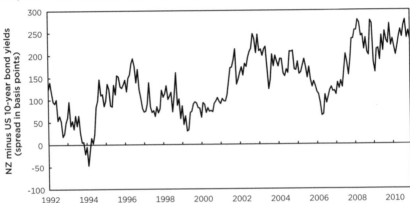

Source: RBNZ, DataStream
NZ 10-year government bond yield: RBNZ, Table B2
US 10-year government bond yield: DataStream, USAGLTB
Note: There are 100 basis points to 1 percentage point.

New Zealand's country risk premium is the difference between the interest rate that investors require to buy, for example, New Zealand ten-year government bonds and the interest rate they are prepared to accept to buy equivalent US bonds. The premium is expressed in basis points where 100 basis points equal 1 percentage point. Over the period 1992 to 2006 the country risk premium averaged about 100 to 150 basis points. That is to say, investors required an additional 1 to 1.5 per cent interest to buy New Zealand bonds. This premium rose sharply from 2006 to 2008 as a result of the onset of the GFC in 2007. The GFC was precipitated by a 'flight from risk' in global capital markets, and since New Zealand is seen as a risky place to invest in, the premium rose.

By definition, the value of liabilities in a balance sheet must equal the value of assets, and the residual item ensuring this parity in Table 7.2 is 'shareholders' funds'. This figure represents the net worth of the institution to its owners – those who carry the risks but also enjoy a share in the profits. Because it is the interest on bank loans that generates profits for the institution, there is an obvious incentive for the bank to increase the amount of credit it issues. There are, however, two significant constraints on this incentive.

The first constraint is that depositors are able to withdraw cash from the bank at any time. But, as Table 7.2 illustrates, the value of cash and other liquid assets held by the institution may be considerably less than the value of its customers' deposits. In order to maintain confidence in its soundness, and to avoid having to sell some of its loan portfolio if there is a 'run on the bank' by its depositors, the bank must maintain a prudent 'reserve asset ratio' of liquid assets to deposits. In the example shown in Table 7.2, the reserve asset ratio is the sum of the first three assets ($150 million) divided by the value of deposits ($750 million) – that is, 20 per cent.

The second constraint is that the value of shareholders' funds is vulnerable to bad debts. Suppose, for example, that a major fall in property values caused a series of bankruptcies among the borrowers in Table 7.2, who then defaulted on their debts to the value of $70 million. This 10 per cent fall in the value of the institution's loans would reduce its total assets to $930 million. The value of deposits would be unaffected, so shareholders' funds would be reduced to $110 million, which is almost a 40 per cent fall in the value of the owners' equity. Again, to maintain confidence in the institution, the value of shareholders' funds must be sufficient to cover any such episode of serious bad debts. This ability is measured by capital adequacy ratios, which record the ratio of shareholders' funds to a risk-weighted measure of the bank's assets. In Table 7.2, for example, a simple capital adequacy ratio is the ratio of shareholders' funds ($180 million) to loans to customers ($730 million) – that is, 25 per cent.

Registered banks in New Zealand are highly rated by world standards, with capital adequacy ratios of around 8 per cent (not the 25 per cent shown in the stylised example above, Table 7.2). Lower-rated banks in Europe and the US had capital adequacy ratios of less than 8 per cent during the GFC. In the lead-up to the crisis some other types of banks, including investment banks, had even lower capital adequacy ratios and this was one reason why many of these banks had to be bailed out by governments.

An added vulnerability of banks and other financial institutions is the short-term structure of some borrowing from global money markets. New Zealand banks and other financial institutions borrowed liberally from these markets. Until recently, this borrowing tended to be on a short-term basis and was used to provide mortgages for property buyers in a booming real estate market.

When a bank is lending money long term for land and property investments its profits are vulnerable to unexpected rises in the cost of borrowed funds. This was a major issue during the GFC in 2007/08 when the wholesale markets for bank funds stopped working for brief periods – banks were unable to borrow at any price. In almost any other sector a brief market freeze would not constitute a crisis, but in financial markets a freeze can cause the whole payments system to shut down. In New Zealand's case, the Reserve Bank intervened quickly to make money available to banks so that their operations were not interrupted during the crisis. Some bank depositors were so concerned that they withdrew all their money in cash – luckily, the Reserve Bank had a large supply of $100 notes that it could make available at short notice for just this purpose. Such behaviour is a reminder of the importance of confidence in the financial system.

There are a number of other deposit-taking financial institutions in New Zealand including some finance companies. The principles underlying their operations are similar to those of the registered banks just described above. However, unlike banks, they are not an integral part of the payments system infrastructure and they are more lightly regulated by the Reserve Bank. Other deposit-taking institutions have failed in New Zealand much more regularly than registered banks, and government is currently exploring ways to make this sector more stable.

FINANCIAL INTERMEDIARY RISKS

Financial intermediaries – banks and non-banks – face particular risks. These risks include a loss of confidence in the system, the risk associated with borrowing short term and lending long term, the failure of another financial intermediary (termed counterparty risk) and the risk of a bank run. These risks need to be understood to ensure the smooth operation of the economy.

The first risk is a loss of confidence in the financial system. Because the larger banks are integral to the payments and settlement infrastructure, a failure in any one of them would threaten the whole system. Other financial institutions in New Zealand, such as finance companies, building societies and investment banks, are less important to the payments and settlement system. This banking environment stands in contrast to the situation in large foreign financial centres. In the US and Europe non-deposit-taking investment banks and even large insurance companies have become highly interconnected with deposit-taking banks so that even non-deposit-taking firms like the American Insurance Group (AIG), J.P. Morgan and Goldman Sachs were seen as too big to fail during the GFC and were bailed out by governments. The investment bank Lehman Brothers was an exception and allowed to go bankrupt.

The second risk is from duration mismatch. A policy of borrowing short term and lending long term is inherently risky unless a bank can convince depositors that it is carefully screening prospective borrowers and monitoring the progress of the loans. When a bank is also relying on foreign sources of funds there will be occasions like 2008 when the supply of funds is interrupted.

A third risk highlighted in the GFC is counterparty risk. The smooth operation of the economy's payments and settlement system requires that banks are prepared to lend to one another as well as to investors. A breakdown in this wholesale market lending can have a domino effect and cause weaker banks to fail if they can't get short-term funding from the market.

A fourth risk is a bank run – a sharp decline in bank trust by depositors who try to withdraw all their money at once. During the GFC, depositors queued outside branches of the Northern Rock Bank in the UK in a run on the bank.

In New Zealand the Reserve Bank regulates capital adequacy and exercises other oversight measures over financial intermediaries to address these risks and ensure that the financial system does not fail. Responding to the GFC, the Reserve Bank introduced a core funding ratio restriction (CFR) in 2010 requiring banks to find 65 per cent of their funds from stable sources in New Zealand. Stable sources are defined as deposits by New Zealand residents or wholesale borrowings with maturities longer than a year. This ratio is planned to rise to 75 per cent by 2012.

One of the ways financial intermediaries attempt to imbue trust in the market is to pay rating agencies such as Fitch and Standard and Poor's to grade products like corporate bonds and the strength of their institutions. The rating agencies themselves have been facing public scrutiny since the GFC because they gave high ratings to some of the complex financial products that proved unsaleable during the flight from risk in 2007. The rating agencies are private firms and their profitability is dependent on their reputations. However, their profitability is also dependent on collecting fees from the firms they are rating.

There are elements of 'moral hazard' in financial markets – situations where people change their behaviour because the risks associated with their actions are carried by somebody else. For example, holders of fire insurance policies are likely to be less careful about lighting fires. New Zealand has attempted to deal with moral hazard in particular ways.

First, lenders in New Zealand have the right to sue borrowers if they cannot continue to meet their obligations. This contrasts with the situation in many US states where house mortgages are non-recourse loans – the bank is limited to taking the house, but not other assets, in the event of non-payment. In New Zealand, borrowers have a greater incentive to meet obligations on house loans and negotiate with lenders if payments become too onerous.

Second, New Zealand bank deposits have not traditionally been guaranteed by government. In this environment, depositors had an incentive to monitor the creditworthiness of banks – not an easy task.

THE NEW ZEALAND ECONOMY

New Zealand and Australia were among the few countries to adopt this policy. However, when Australia announced it would introduce deposit guarantees during the GFC, New Zealand followed suit to prevent a flight of bank deposits to Australia. Retail deposit guarantees were extended until the end of 2011 but most banks opted out of the scheme in late 2010, probably because it was expensive to belong to and they believed customers have confidence in their management.

INFLATION CONTROL

One of the key elements of macroeconomic stability is price stability or inflation control. Periods of rapidly rising or falling prices (inflation or deflation) tend to reflect unstable economic growth. Monetary policy refers to actions by the Reserve Bank that influence interest rates and, through that mechanism, money supply, exchange rates, economic activity, employment and inflation.

Inflation distorts incentives and economic activity. If prices are rising, then a dollar earned and saved today will buy less tomorrow and investment values will be eroded if inflation outstrips the return on investment. In periods of sustained inflation businesses and households make fewer long-term investments. Reduced investment cuts the economy's growth potential.

Deflation can also be damaging. When prices are falling, firms and households will put off expenditure as they will be able to buy cheaper in the future. Deflation is unusual, but the Japanese economy has been deflating now for 20 years with accompanying poor economic performance.

Government policy changes often require trade-offs. Controlling inflation requires, at least in the short term, a trade-off with unemployment. The Phillips Curve, discovered by the New Zealand economist Bill Phillips, shows that when inflation rises, unemployment falls in the short term, and vice versa. Too much inflation is undesirable, as discussed above. However, if inflation is reduced by choking economic growth, this will lead to a temporary rise in unemployment. Accordingly, the Reserve Bank is implicitly charged with the delicate task of balancing inflation and unemployment.

Inflation is caused by too much money available in the economy chasing too few goods and driving prices up. Up until the 1980s, New Zealand attempts to keep inflation low therefore focused on regulating the quantity of money in the system. Government regulated the banking reserve ratios in order to control the volume of loans issued by banks and finance companies. When inflationary pressures emerged, government would raise the reserve ratio on loans for, say, car purchases. During this period the exchange rate was also fixed by government which made it very difficult to stop importing inflation from major trading partners. After the exchange rate was fully floated in March 1985 government introduced a new monetary policy regime which has evolved over time to the present system of manipulating not the quantity of money but its price – interest rates.

The Reserve Bank is required to maintain price stability under the Reserve Bank of New Zealand Act 1989. A separate Policy Targets Agreement (PTA) between the governor of the Reserve Bank and the Minister of Finance is negotiated when the governor is appointed (or reappointed). The latest PTA requires the Reserve Bank to maintain inflation, as measured by the annual increase in the consumer price index, between 1 and 3 per cent on average in the medium term. The PTA may be changed at any time by government but it has to be changed publicly. This makes monetary policy very transparent, with fewer surprises for financial markets. The PTA also passes full responsibility for the conduct of monetary policy to the governor. The Reserve Bank is allowed to 'look through' (ignore) short-term price volatility associated with policy changes (e.g. an increase in the GST rate in October 2010) or price shocks (e.g. oil price increases in global markets). Accordingly, the Reserve Bank pursues price stability coupled with economic, exchange rate and financial market stability.

The Reserve Bank's main tool is the Official Cash Rate (OCR). You will recall that the Reserve Bank provides an important component of the inter-bank payments and settlement system each night via the trading bank accounts at the Bank. It has a monopoly on bank settlement accounts for a number of reasons. First, the Reserve Bank is the only legal issuer of notes and coins and is paid in money held in the settlement cash accounts. Second, the Bank acts as the banker for the government and requires that the transactions with the government (e.g. taxes, welfare payments, student allowances, etc.) be made in settlement cash. Third, the Reserve Bank's almost risk-free credit rating means that banks reduce their counterparty risk by settling inter-bank transactions via the Bank.

These accounts for daily settlement must stay in credit but the Reserve Bank will buy government bonds from the banks that are near settlement date if the cash reserves in their Reserve Bank account are insufficient on a particular night. However, these bond sales are carried out at a discount determined by the OCR. The OCR is, accordingly, the minimum interest rate for all inter-bank credit dealings. All other interest rates are set above the OCR by the bank margins required in particular segments of the capital markets. The governor of the Reserve Bank assesses economic conditions every six weeks and decides on the appropriate level of the OCR.

Graph 7.5 **Nominal interest rates, 1990–2010**

Source: RBNZ
Floating mortgage rate: RBNZ, Table B3
Interbank cash rate: RBNZ, Table B2
Official cash rate: RBNZ, Table B2

Graph 7.5 illustrates recent changes in the OCR and the effect on floating mortgage interest rates. From 2003 the New Zealand economy experienced inflationary pressures resulting from faster GDP growth. Rising property prices were also expected to be inflationary, because when people feel wealthier, they spend more. The OCR was accordingly raised from 5 per cent to 8.25 per cent. Mortgage interest rates rose in lock-step to over 10 per cent. When the OCR was reduced to 2.5 per cent in 2009, mortgage rates followed it down but not to the same extent, because bank costs for borrowed funds were rising as a result of the higher foreign risk premium.

When the Reserve Bank seeks to cool inflation, it raises interest rates. This essentially reduces the demand for goods and services relative to supply, which dampens inflation. The reduction in demand works through a number of channels. First, savings are encouraged by higher deposit rates. Second, borrowing and investment is discouraged through the higher cost of funds. Together, money is reallocated from consumption to saving and investment is reduced. A higher interest rate will also typically lead to an appreciation in the exchange rate. The higher exchange rate reduces exports as each unit of exports now earns the New Zealand producer less. So, a rise in the interest rate leads to a reduction in consumption, investment and exports. As economic activity is reduced, so too is employment, wage growth and inflation.

When the Reserve Bank seeks to stimulate the economy and inflation, it reduces interest rates. That encourages consumption over savings, and borrowing for investment. A lower exchange rate will also support exports. These outcomes will result in higher economic activity, employment, wage growth and inflation.

Changes in the OCR do not affect behaviour immediately. Interest rate changes typically take one to two years to have their full impact on economic activity and inflation. The Reserve Bank has to look ahead in formulating monetary policy based on forecasts and judgement. The lag between OCR changes and their impact on the economy depends on a range of factors. In the period 2007 to 2009, during which the Reserve Bank raised the OCR significantly, the impact on the economy was low.

The main reason was that most mortgages were fixed for two years or more. So, while mortgage rates rose, the impact on borrowers was small until they refinanced their fixed mortgages.

Retail interest rates are also affected by the cost of borrowing money offshore. Always provided that funds are available to New Zealand borrowers, the cost of offshore funds is the interest rate in the international financial centre (Tokyo, New York, London or Zurich) plus the New Zealand country risk premium mentioned earlier. Banks will be prepared to pay New Zealand residents the opportunity cost of borrowing offshore for term deposits and other domestic borrowing. At the time of writing, the cost of offshore funds and term deposits in New Zealand was significantly higher than the OCR so the gap between the OCR and retail mortgage rates is higher than in the past, Graph 7.5.

CONCLUSION

The capital market is an important arena for matching savers and investors. This includes direct investments, such as shares, bonds and property. Other financial intermediaries like banks, finance companies and building societies perform a similar task, by taking in deposits and giving out credit. Interest rates are a key parameter in savings and investment activity.

The Reserve Bank changes interest rates through the capital markets to tilt the balance between savings and investment, maintain price stability and smooth out fluctuations in the economy. When the economy is growing quickly and inflation is rising, the Reserve Bank raises the OCR in order to cool the economy. Conversely, it lowers the OCR to stimulate the economy when the economy is in recession and inflation is low.

8 Government sector and fiscal policy

The government (or public) sector is a large part of the New Zealand economy. Government expenditure represents over a third of GDP. Government has three economic roles: to promote an efficient allocation of resources (including by providing public goods); to ensure a fair distribution of income; and to provide macroeconomic stability.

There are three levels of government in New Zealand: central government administered by Parliament; district and city councils; and regional councils. The focus of this chapter is on central government because it is the largest economic component of the public sector and it occupies the senior role in decision-making.

FISCAL POLICY

Fiscal policy refers to the incentives the government provides for the economy. These include how the government collects revenue (different types of taxes and excises) and how it spends it (health, education, security, etc.). Fiscal policy is not only about what is taxed and spent, but also how these functions are carried out. The 'what' impacts on the economy in the short run. For example, if the government spends more than it taxes, then it will be injecting money into the economy and boosting economic activity. This may entail the government running down savings, or borrowing. The 'how' of fiscal policy is also very important. For example, the government can raise revenue through personal income tax or through goods and services tax. One taxes income and the other taxes consumption. By taxing one more than the other, the government can create an incentive for households to work harder and consume less.

The economics of the government sector differs from the economics of the private or market economy by virtue of its status and consequent powers. Democratic states give governments strong powers of coercion that are not permitted in other organisations. Governments can compulsorily tax residents. They have the power to set many of the rules that govern economic life.

The decision-making processes of democratic government in economic affairs also differ significantly from market interactions between firms and households. This is the subject of political economy and public economics. Politicians form themselves into political parties which attempt to gain or retain power by building constituencies of private sector interests. These interests, in turn, form associations or lobby groups to influence government decision-making. This lobby group activity is often 'rent-seeking' behaviour because it attempts to gain special economic rewards (rents) for its own associates.

Part of the growth in government over time is associated with countering these lobbying influences by establishing advisory bodies (ministries) to provide independent advice to government on policy matters as well as departments to carry out policy. Those ministries have in turn established other external agencies to administer parts of government policy or to operate commercial activities that government wants to be involved in. To complicate matters, these government ministries, departments and agencies also tend to develop their own agendas. A large government department has a propensity to want to grow larger – the larger it becomes, the more influence it can have over policy matters and the more prestigious its senior managers become.

The demand for government programmes and policy can be thought of as emanating from lobby groups and public opinion while the supply of policy and programmes arises from the benefits to politicians – usually buffered by ministry advice. It is a form of supply-demand analysis but one that is different from the supply-demand framework used to explain market behaviour.

GOVERNMENT BALANCE SHEET

The balance sheet of government reflects the accumulation of past political decisions in this complex environment. The central government balance sheet as it stood in June 2010 is summarised in Table 8.1. Government had $223 billion of assets and $128 billion of liabilities on that date. The difference ($95 billion) is nominally the amount of 'shareholder' funds that accrue to the nation as a whole. Total government assets are around 40 per cent of the total value of shares listed on the New Zealand Stock Exchange. Government assets are a much smaller share of total private sector assets, which include private land, housing and farms.

The largest asset category is property, plant and equipment, $113 billion. This includes the value of state highways, electric power plants, government buildings and the railways. It is spread fairly evenly between the property assets of core government departments (Treasury, the State Services Commission and the Ministries of Economic Development, Health, Agriculture and Forestry, Work and Income, Justice, etc.), crown entities (e.g. Te Papa, ACC, Radio New Zealand, the EQC, the Crown Research Institutes, the New Zealand Symphony Orchestra) and state-owned enterprises (e.g. Solid Energy, New Zealand Railways Corporation, Transpower, Meridian Energy, Landcorp and New Zealand Post).

The second-largest category, marketable securities and deposits, includes the value of the New Zealand Superannuation Fund ($15.7 billion), Reserve Bank assets ($23.5 billion), the ACC portfolio ($13.7 billion) and the Earthquake Commission portfolio ($6 billion, which is likely to decline, to meet insurance payments following the devastating earthquakes in Canterbury in 2010 and 2011).

Table 8.1 **New Zealand government balance sheet, June 2010**

Balance sheet	$m
Assets	
Cash & cash equivalents	7,774
Receivables	13,884
Marketable securities, deposits & derivatives in gain	43,687
Share investments	12,179
Advances	18,447
Inventory	1,160
Other assets	1,661
Property, plant & equipment	113,330
Equity accounted investments	9,049
Intangible assets & goodwill	2,184
Total assets	223,355
Liabilities	
Issued currency	4,020
Payables	9,931
Deferred revenue	1,628
Borrowings	69,733
Insurance liabilities	27,131
Retirement plan liabilities	9,940
Provisions	5,984
Total liabilities	128,367

Source: New Zealand Treasury, Financial Statements of the Government of New Zealand: for the year ended June 2010, 978-0-478-35071-5

The next asset category in the list is share investments ($12 billion). This includes the government shareholding in Air New Zealand. The following item, advances of $18.4 billion, incorporates diverse assets including student loans ($6.8 billion), Kiwibank mortgages ($10.4 billion) and New Zealand deposits with the International Monetary Fund (IMF) of $2.2 billion.

On the liabilities side, the stock of government gross debt (borrowings) is the largest category at $69.7 billion. This stock figure is often expressed relative to GDP, as in Graph 8.4. It approximates the nation's ability to service outstanding government debt, as GDP approximates national income.

Government debt has declined markedly relative to GDP in recent decades. This was one of New Zealand's economic strengths in the aftermath of the Global Financial Crisis, because government debt in many other countries had risen sharply after governments were forced to bail out banks and other financial institutions. Nevertheless, the New Zealand government debt ratio began to rise again in 2010 and Treasury has forecast that it will keep rising until 2015.

The second-largest liability in Table 8.1 is insurance liabilities ($27.1 billion). This item is almost entirely comprised of ACC liabilities for future claims ($27 billion).

GOVERNMENT EXPENDITURE

While the balance sheet records the net asset position of government, its revenue and expenditure accounts record the flow of financial resources to and from government over a period of time. Here we deviate from the classifications used in the government balance sheet above and focus only on core government activities. Core activities exclude the revenue and expenditure of state-owned enterprises and crown entities, as they are usually run as independent organisations and their revenue and expenditure cannot be used as policy instruments (like raising taxes to increase revenue or cutting welfare to reduce expenditure).

The major categories of core government expenditure and core revenue for the year ending June 2010 are given in Tables 8.2 and 8.3. In the year to June 2010, the New Zealand government spent $64 billion on core activities, Table 8.2. Seventy-two per cent of this total was spent on social security, health and education services.

The pattern of government expenditure has changed significantly since the 1970s. Prior to the economic reforms of 1984, a higher proportion of government expenditure was devoted to economic and industrial services. This took the form of export and production subsidies. Nevertheless, government still provides $7.5 billion of economic and industrial services. Over the past decade, for example, government has provided grants of over $200 million for big-budget films made in New Zealand and grants or subsidies for sporting events, tourism development, meat marketing and other ventures.

Table 8.2 **Government expenditure by category, year ending June 2010**

Expenditure	$m
Social security & welfare	21,185
Health	13,128
Education	11,724
Core government services	2,974
Law & order	3,191
Defence	1,771
Other core services	7,263
Finance costs	2,777
Core crown expenses	64,013
Crown entities, others & SOEs	17,027
Total crown expenses	81,040

Source: New Zealand Treasury, Financial Statements of the Government of New Zealand: for the year ended June 2010, 978-0-478-35071-5

The activities associated with the assets listed in the balance sheet (Table 8.1) are often not the same as the activities encompassed by the expenditure accounts. The government owns and operates some functions, while it outsources others – that is, governments face 'make' or 'buy' options. Take government involvement in education as an example. The balance sheet includes the value of all schools and educational institutions owned by the state. The expenditure accounts include the costs of running these state-owned establishments – the 'make' or government provision portion. The expenditure accounts also include the cost of 'buying' other education services from private schools and universities that the state does not own. Government does this by subsidising private institutions to provide the services government wants from the private sector (in addition, in this case, to government provision). It is not appropriate to include the capital value of private schools in the government balance sheet, so both the balance sheet and expenditure account are important in analysing education policy.

Government is involved in many other markets in New Zealand, aside from the market for education services. Sometimes, like education, government is the major provider. Airline services, pensions, power generation, conservation and heritage, health, insurance (ACC, Work and Income and EQC), coal mining (Solid Energy), roading, social welfare, security and quality control services are other areas where there is a high level of government involvement. Sometimes government assumes a monopoly position in a market – as in the provision of railway services, courts, national defence, central banking and tax collection services. In other markets, government assumes a minority presence, as in retail banking services (Kiwibank) and farming (Landcorp and DOC).

There will always be political debate about how active governments need to be in each of these areas. Conservatives will argue that past governments run by opposition parties have intervened too much in certain areas and that intervention needs to be lightened. Social democrats will argue that the high level of intervention they instituted was about right. One of the political objectives of all parties will be to appeal to the median voter, because without that support they cannot gain or maintain power.

If you consider the long list of government market interventions just given, it is not always clear whether government is targeting one of the three economic roles or some other objective. Indeed, 'political expediency' is sometimes the only way to rationalise interventions. All the same, New Zealand governments have made important efforts in recent decades to limit ad hoc policy interventions. Successive administrations have been at pains to constrain their own actions through the Monetary Targets Agreement on monetary policy and the Fiscal Responsibility Act on government expenditure and revenue.

The trend in government core expenditure since 1972 is given in Graph 8.1. Expenditure rose rapidly as a proportion of GDP over the 1970s as government attempted to buffer the effects of the oil shocks on private consumption. Expenditure continued to climb during the economic reform period as unemployment rose to post-war record levels in 1992. Thereafter expenditure fell sharply relative to GDP, as the economy recovered from the reforms after 1992. The incoming Labour government in 1999 introduced a range of new expenditure programmes that resulted in core expenditure rising from around 30 per cent of GDP in 2004 to nearly 35 per cent in 2010.

Graph 8.1 **Government expenditure, 1972–2010**

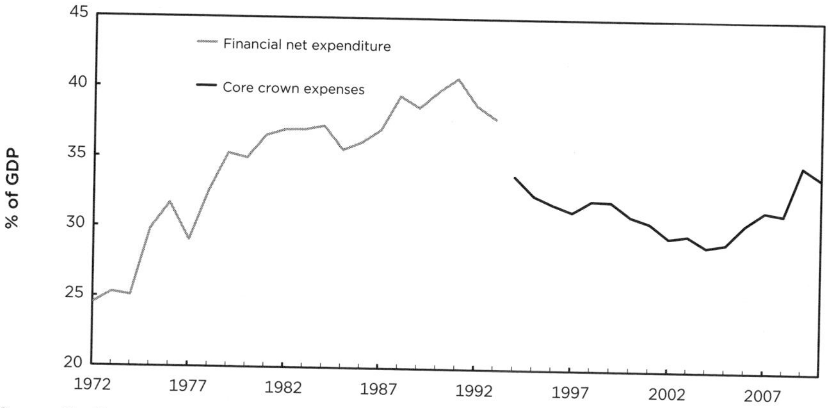

Source: The Treasury, Historical Fiscal Indicators 1972–2010, published by the Treasury at http://www.treasury.govt.nz/government/data

These longer-term trends reflect differences in political preferences. Labour and National governments from 1984 to 1999 broadly embraced a philosophy of a 'more market' economy and generally sought to restrict expenditure and improve the allocation of resources across the economy. There was greater reliance on the market economy providing goods and services. However, the economic reform programme and its consequent dislocations built up significant public opposition. This discord was reinforced by the growing disparity in wages and income between higher and lower deciles of households. Accordingly, the Labour government elected in 1999 sought to respond to this political feeling by expanding programmes and associated expenditure relative to GDP.

There are three areas of government expenditure where over a longer period governments have been unable to find a sustainable political consensus: pensions, health and education. The political conflict in these areas has led to almost continuous policy change in the government programmes involved. This vacillation has resulted in government expenditure in these areas trending upwards in an unsustainable fashion – unsustainable because the root causes of the issues involved are not being dealt with.

For example, New Zealand governments have had a long tradition of providing public health-care services and public education services at zero cost or very low cost to users. This arrangement makes the services more accessible to people on low incomes and it greatly increases the demand for those services by people on higher incomes. This universal access policy receives strong political support because it combines the influence of lobbies for the poor with the median voter lobbies – the latter being the political power brokers in a democracy (Hotelling's Law).

However, the universal provision approach has proven to be unsustainable because the inevitable rationing systems (introduced to constrain government expenditure to reasonable levels) eventually become unpopular and have to be replaced by new rationing systems. The new system is itself soon criticised as inefficient or inequitable and the policy cycle begins again. Health services are especially difficult for the state to provide universally because the demand for these services rises quickly in conjunction with higher incomes and technological progress in the health sector. For example, the advent of CT scanners means many patients will now get a costly but more informative CT scan in addition to an X-ray. Such duplication adds to the rising medical costs associated with technological change.

The universality approach tends to penalise lower-income people for two reasons. First, if a government programme is available to everyone, then most of the resources will be devoted to middle-income groups, leaving fewer resources to be devoted to the poor. Secondly, middle- and higher-income people are often better able to capture benefits from a universal system. They are better educated and better connected socially, so they are more likely to be able to discover the inevitable 'chinks' in the rationing system. Some years ago a survey of the British public health system, another universal health system, found that 80 per cent of the health services available went to 20 per cent of the population – the highest-income earners. Universal government programmes might be egalitarian in the view of some but they tend to redistribute income from the poor to the rich. The power of the median voter is a major challenge for social development.

GOVERNMENT REVENUE

The sources of government revenue for the year ending June 2010 are given in Table 8.3. The largest source is income tax levied on individuals. Income tax is levied on all income from wages, salaries and profits but not on income earned from long-term capital gains. It is levied on individual taxpayers rather than households. The tax is subject to a number of offsets that provide relief for people on low incomes, for households with dependent children and for households who can use trusts and company structures to avoid the highest rates of income tax. For these reasons New Zealand governments have put increasing emphasis on consumption taxes rather than income taxes.

The second-largest source of revenue is from New Zealand's unusually broadly based consumption tax – the goods and services tax (GST). This tax was introduced at a rate of 10 per cent in 1986 during the economic reform period and offset by a large reduction in the maximum income tax rate from 66 per cent to 33 per cent. GST was quickly raised to 12.5 per cent in 1989, and then to 15 per cent in October 2010. One of the strengths of the GST regime is that it is applied to virtually all goods and services. Exceptions include rents and financial services. This breadth of application is a strength of the tax in political economy terms. It strengthens the political will of governments to resist making further exemptions.

Politicians find it very difficult to resist pressures to accommodate the demands of lobby groups for special status if exceptions have been previously granted. Consumption taxes in other countries often have a number of exemptions that cause firms to alter the form of their products and cause consumers to change their consumption patterns to accommodate different tax rates. This results in an added burden of the tax (economic inefficiencies). One classic example of successive governments accommodating requests for exemptions to a tax is the import tariff. In the 1830s the governor of New Zealand introduced a single import tariff of 10 per cent. Today, there are thousands of different import tariffs – the tariff manual extends to over 2000 pages!

Table 8.3 **Government revenue by category, year ending June 2010**

Revenue	$m
Individuals	24,050
Corporate tax	7,901
Other direct income tax	1,949
GST	11,341
Excises & other indirect taxes	4,863
Other revenue	6,112
Core crown expenses	56,216
Crown entities, others & SOEs	18,509
Core crown revenue	74,725

Source: New Zealand Treasury, Financial Statements of the Government of New Zealand: for the year ended June 2010, 978-0-478-35071-5

The third-largest source of tax revenue is corporate income tax. This tax is paid by the shareholders of companies. It does not involve double taxation as in the past, where the business pays tax on profits and then the investor pays tax on any dividends paid out from this after-tax profit. Corporate income tax is essentially a tax on the capital owned by shareholders. The levels of corporate tax on capital and income taxes levied on labour have become an increasingly important issue. In a globalised world, workers and capital are both internationally mobile. Higher taxes may result in outflows of labour and capital to the detriment of production in New Zealand. This is one of the reasons the 2010 Budget reduced income and corporate tax rates and replaced the lost revenue by increasing the goods and services tax. The effectiveness

THE NEW ZEALAND ECONOMY

of this policy switch remains to be seen as the decision to stay or set up business in New Zealand also depends on a range of other factors like size of the market and opportunities for growth.

Graph 8.2 **Government revenue, 1972–2010**

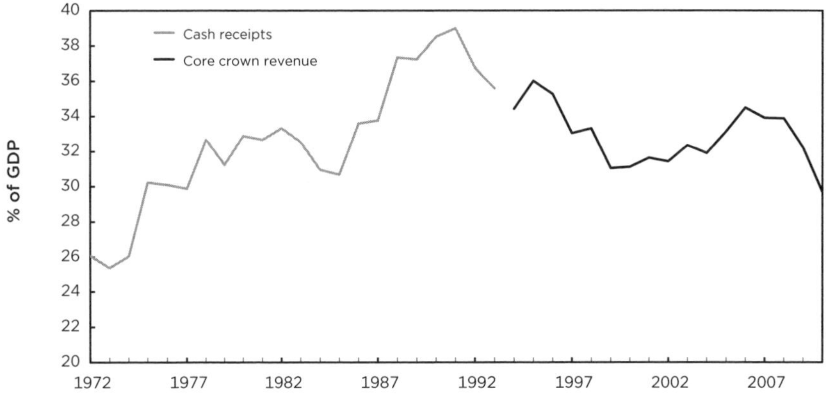

Source: The Treasury, Historical Fiscal Indicators 1972–2010, published by the Treasury at http://www.treasury.govt.nz/government/data

Excise taxes on petrol and tobacco products raised $4.9 billion in 2010 with other revenue raised from royalties on mineral exploration, gift taxes and interest on investments. Notably, New Zealand has no death duties or capital gains taxes and it is planned to abolish gift taxes in 2011.

The pattern of government revenue over time (Graph 8.2) broadly mirrors the pattern of government expenditure (Graph 8.1) but the differences in levels are important. These differences are shown more clearly in Graph 8.3 as the fiscal balance. The large increases in government expenditure during the 1970s were not matched by similar increases in revenue because government wanted to boost household income at a time of weak export prices and high import prices. The fiscal deficit deteriorated sharply to reach over 6 per cent of GDP. The economic reform programme of the following decade reduced this deficit position and a fiscal surplus was achieved in the early 1990s. The surplus continued until 2007 when New Zealand entered a period of recession. Expenditure increased through unemployment benefits and tax revenue declined as a result of lower wages and profits. These adjustments are part of the automatic stabilisation programme of government. The fiscal balance went back into deficit in 2009 and 2010, Graph 8.3.

Graph 8.3 **Fiscal balance, 1972–2010**

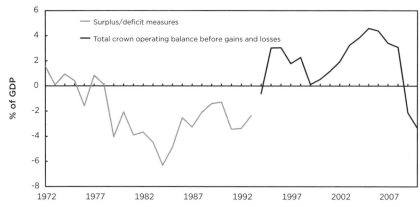

Source: The Treasury, Historical Fiscal Indicators 1972–2010, published by the Treasury at http://www.treasury.govt.nz/government/data

FISCAL BALANCE AND GOVERNMENT DEBT

In 2010, core government revenue was $56.2 billion or $7.8 billion less than core government expenditure, Tables 8.2 and 8.3. The difference in total (not just core) revenue and expenditure is a little smaller: expenditure exceeded revenue by $6.3 billion.

The fiscal balance in a particular year represents a change in the level of government debt. It is interesting to get some perspective on the history of government debt in New Zealand, Graph 8.4. In 1900, gross government debt was around 125 per cent of New Zealand GDP. Government was very active at this point in New Zealand history with investments in ports, railways, banking and other sectors. The onset of World War I imposed high costs on government and the war was partially financed through borrowing which added to gross debt. This was compounded by the cost of dealing with the Great Depression from

1929 and again borrowing was used extensively to finance job creation and other programmes. Gross government debt reached 250 per cent of GDP by 1935.

Graph 8.4 **Government debt, 1900-2010**

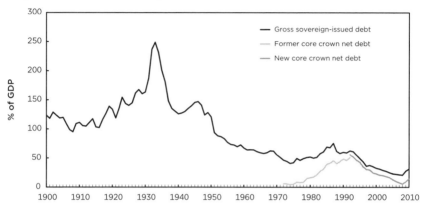

Source: RBNZ, The Treasury
1900-1970 gross debt: Reddell and Sleeman (2008)
1970-current for all indicators: Historical Fiscal Indicators 1972-2010,
published by the Treasury at http://www.treasury.govt.nz/government/data

After 1935, gross debt declined almost continuously with three exceptions. The cost of financing New Zealand's participation in World War II caused gross debt to rise by about 20 percentage points in the 1940s. It rose by a similar percentage in the 1970s and 1980s in government's attempt to buffer the effects of the first two oil shocks. Finally, government gross debt started to rise again in 2008 in the aftermath of the GFC and a New Zealand recession, but from a very low base.

There is currently a concern that government debt may continue to rise from its turning point in 2008 and increase to unsustainable levels in the decades ahead, Graph 8.5. Treasury forecasts that net government debt could rise from current levels of 10 per cent of GDP to around 200 per cent of GDP by 2050 unless action is taken to change a number of important government expenditure programmes, particularly in the areas of health and pensions.

The New Zealand population is ageing, even if not to the extent found in many other developed economies. This has implications for projected government expenditure in a number of areas. Health care for the elderly is much more expensive than for younger people. The cost of state pensions will also rise in an ageing population because superannuation is not means tested and is wage-level adjusted, rather than tied to consumer prices which rise at a slower pace.

Graph 8.5 **Government net debt projections, 2010–2050**

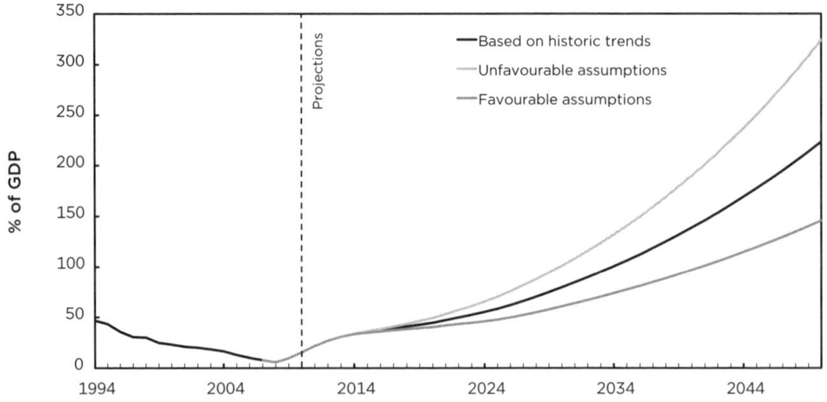

Source: The Treasury Long Term Fiscal Model (2010),
available at: http://www.treasury.govt.nz/government/longterm/fiscalmodel/ltfm-ltfs09.xls

The economic cost of taxation in New Zealand is also expected to rise in the future because taxation is not inflation adjusted. Accordingly, nominal wage rises are expected to result in tax increases that are proportionately larger than the wage increases. For example, unless income tax brackets are altered in future, the lowest-paid workers will be in the maximum tax bracket of 33 per cent within 40 years. There will be considerable pressure for tax brackets to be adjusted to account for this taxation creep in the future.

On a basis of projected population and participation rates, and linear productivity growth, Treasury has made the government debt projections shown in Graph 8.5. This is a relatively simple projection framework – a range of known feedback loops are ignored in the interests of simplicity. Nonetheless, the projections are robust enough to serve as a discussion starter on future government revenue and expenditure policy.

CONCLUSION

The government sector plays an important role in the economy. It provides the institutional frameworks for the economy, such as rules, regulations and their application through agencies such as courts, police and the Department of Labour. Government also sets the incentives for the economy, through taxes and spending.

If the government spends more than it gathers from the economy, usually through taxes, then this will stimulate economic growth. However, spending more than revenue gathered means either savings have to be run down or the funds borrowed. So, this is not a long-term solution to supporting economic growth. Instead, governments need to settle on a balanced set of institutions and incentives.

9 Macroeconomic forecasting

INTRODUCTION

Forecasting the future performance of the economy is a mix of science and art. The economy is complex and its parts are interrelated. As a result, simplified models of the economy often require judgements to reflect current economic trends and likely surprises. However, unexpected events often occur and cannot be accounted for ahead of time.

In spite of the difficulties, forecasts are essential for many institutions – they have to have a view of the future. Forecasts provide a baseline scenario for planning purposes for businesses, government and the Reserve Bank of New Zealand. Businesses will not invest in new capacity, hire more staff or pay higher wages unless they think there will be sufficient demand for their products to recoup their investments. The government needs to know the outlook for the economy so that it can budget for expenditure and revenue collection. The Reserve Bank needs to forecast economic activity to formulate a view on the likelihood of inflation or an economic slowdown.

In using forecasts it is essential to understand that each of the numbers produced is the mid-point of a range. In other words, each point forecast is surrounded by a standard error. Forecasters attempt to incorporate all current information and the likely future direction of economic drivers. They try to account for known uncertainties such as the direction of interest rates. However, there are also 'unknown' uncertainties like the Global Financial Crisis – the timing and severity of which could not have been predicted with accuracy beforehand.

For all these reasons it is helpful to appreciate the extent of past forecast errors. Forecasters need to evaluate their past errors in order to improve forecasting systems. Graph 9.1 illustrates past GDP forecast errors in New Zealand. The forecasts of GDP in the graph are so-called consensus forecasts – the average of past forecasts made by the major forecasting institutions. The graph clearly shows that forecasters are routinely taken by surprise.

For example, the line labelled 2009 in Graph 9.1 shows the progression in consensus forecasts from October 2008 to the final forecast of the 2009 year in December 2009. In October 2008, forecasters expected the New Zealand economy to grow by plus 1.3 per cent in 2009. By July 2009 they had revised this forecast down to minus 2.2 per cent and in the end the economy contracted by minus 1.7 per cent. Unquestionably, forecasts can be quite inaccurate. However, if you examine the sequence of forecasts for 2000 in Graph 9.2 you will see that forecasters did a better job for that year.

Consensus forecasting is thought to be a useful exercise, as it provides estimates based on all the information that a range of forecasters can bring to bear on an issue at a particular point in time. The GFC was a surprise and subsequent policy responses averted the worst-case outcome in the short term.

As explained in Chapter 1, the macroeconomy is an interrelated system – the influences are circular and there are feedback loops. For example, higher household incomes will initially lead to higher consumption, higher domestic production and/or imports to provide the goods. This supply response will involve more transport and warehousing, more jobs and upward pressure on the cost of these items. As a result, the Reserve Bank may have to raise interest rates. This policy response will slow growth in wages, consumption and the wider economy. The forecaster's task is to analyse the scenario and come to a view as to the likely outcome.

Most macroeconomic forecasters in New Zealand focus on a future horizon of up to five years. For longer periods, the level of uncertainty becomes so large that forecasts of economic cycles lose value. The discussion in the following sections deals mainly with forecasting the business cycle over a period of up to five years.

Graph 9.1 **Evolution of consensus forecasts, 2000 and 2009**

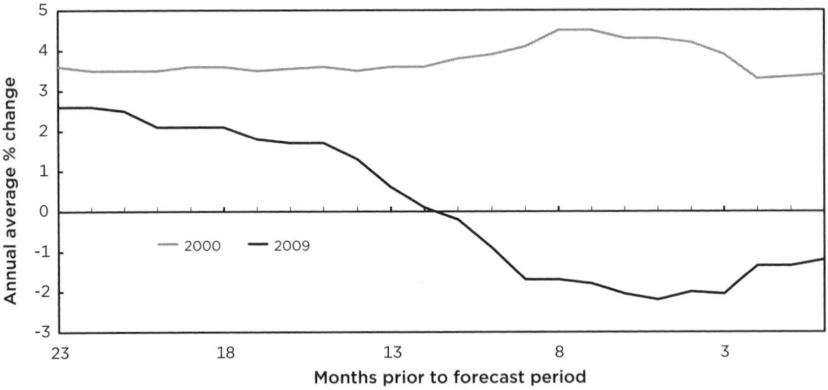

Months prior to forecast period

Source: Consensus Economics

There are, however, instances of longer-term forecasting such as Statistics New Zealand's 50-year forecasts. Over the next 50 years Statistics New Zealand projects the labour force to grow by 0.4 per cent per annum. Treasury has used this forecast to produce the 40-year outlook discussed in Chapter 8. The Treasury model is built around the following logic. Suppose Statistics New Zealand's forecast of labour force growth is correct and that new investment causes the capital stock to increase by 2.5 per cent a year. If labour contributes 75 per cent to GDP and capital 25 per cent, then the weighted average contribution is (0.4 per cent x 0.75) + (2.5 per cent x 0.25) = 0.9 per cent. Assume also that technological advances raise productivity by 1.4 per cent per year (similar to the past two decades), then the long-term real economic growth projection will be (0.9 per cent + 1.4 per cent) = 2.3 per cent per year over their 50-year time horizon.

Note that these longer-term forecasts ignore inevitable business cycles that tend to be the primary focus of most macroeconomic forecasting. However, the strength of the longer-term approach is the focus on important but slower-acting drivers like population and productivity growth.

A BRIEF RECAP OF THE KEY DRIVERS OF THE NEW ZEALAND ECONOMY

Before we get down to the nitty-gritty of forecasting the economy through the business cycle, let's recall the key drivers of the economy. The economy responds to many influences, but these can be boiled down to three main factors:

1. **Monetary policy** – Monetary policy works through interest rates and their impact on savings, borrowing, consumption, investment and exports (through the exchange rate). Every six weeks the Reserve Bank decides on changes in interest rates.
2. **Fiscal policy** – Fiscal policy works through two channels. First, government investment in roads or tax cuts, for example, provides direct injections of money into the economy. Second, government sets the long-term agenda by moulding the incentives to invest, consume and work. The government typically announces policy changes in the May Budget.
3. **Global growth** – We live in a globalised world. The health of the global economy dictates how much we export and at what price, it influences our cost of credit and access to capital and it influences net migration into New Zealand.

THE FORECASTING PROCESS

The key steps in forecasting the economy are:

1. Where have we been?
2. Where are we now?
3. What are the likely changes in policy settings?
4. Forecasting the economy.

Step 1: Where have we been?
The first step in forecasting is to understand economic history. This involves looking at the data to understand what has been driving recent changes in economic activity, whether those drivers will persist or fade, or if there are emerging issues. Economic data is analysed continuously for this purpose.

Longer-term data can also show the impact of past 'shocks'. For example, the impact of the increase in GST on retail spending in October 2010 was assessed by analysing the introduction and subsequent increase in the tax, both in the 1980s. Likewise, the impact of dairy price rises (or falls) on tractor and land sales may be assessed by analysing the effect of past price changes.

Step 2: Where are we now?
An assessment of where the economy is at the time forecasts are being prepared requires a forecast of the current position. Economic data from Statistics New Zealand takes some time to be compiled. For example, GDP data takes around three months – so the March quarter data is released at the end of June. Accordingly, an analyst making a set of forecasts on the first of June has to make an assessment of economic performance from January to May of that year without an official estimate. The forecast will therefore be done by looking at partial and leading indicators to understand the current state of the economy.

1. **House sales** – House sales are a good indicator of household spending, which accounts for around two thirds of total expenditure. If house sales are weak, this generally reflects weak household spending on most goods and services. National house sales data is released by the Real Estate Institute of New Zealand (REINZ) in the first week of the following month.

2. **Net migration** – Accelerating net migration boosts population growth which leads to demand for housing, jobs, goods and services. Higher net migration tends to support stronger growth. Net migration data is compiled by Statistics New Zealand and is typically released in the third week of the following month.

3. **Business and consumer confidence** – Confidence is a necessary but not sufficient condition for businesses to decide to invest, hire and expand. Similarly, consumer confidence can shape people's decisions to buy houses and goods and services. There can be periods of divergence between levels of confidence and actual decisions. This can be the result of a number of factors, including a lack of access to finance to fund investment plans. Monthly business confidence data is released by the National Bank of New Zealand at the end of each month. A more comprehensive survey, the NZIER Quarterly Survey of Business Opinion, is released in the first week following each calendar quarter. Monthly consumer confidence data is released jointly by Roy Morgan and the ANZ Bank. A longer-running quarterly consumer confidence index is published jointly by Westpac and McDermott-Miller.

4. **Commodity prices** – Some rising commodity prices provide a long-term boost to the economy. New Zealand mainly exports agricultural commodities, such as dairy, meat, forestry and horticulture. It is important to note that in the short term only the 10 per cent of the workforce that is employed in the agriculture sector benefits from higher commodity prices while the other 90 per cent of the workforce pays higher prices for their milk, timber, cheese and meat. But commodity prices eventually benefit the wider economy through spending in local communities and

taxes paid to government. The ANZ Bank releases a monthly commodity price index in the first week of the following month.

5. **Stock market performance** – Equity market performance is an excellent indicator of growth. Equity markets tend to rise strongly when the economy is booming and vice versa. For example, equity prices plunged during the GFC, reflecting falling confidence in economic growth. Equity or sharemarket price performance data are freely available from global sites such as Yahoo! Finance and Google Finance, and they are also published in newspapers.

Step 3: What are the likely changes in policy settings?
As noted above in the recap of main drivers of the economy, monetary and fiscal policy settings are two of the key economic drivers. It is possible to get an impression of potential changes in these policy areas ahead of time.

The Reserve Bank decides on the level of interest rates at six-weekly intervals. It releases a statement after each meeting explaining its decision and it provides some commentary on its outlook for the future. This commentary can provide clues on the likely next move in interest rates.

Given the Monetary Policy Framework imposed on the Reserve Bank, the governor will set interest rates according to his or her outlook for future inflation, future economic growth potential and other factors he or she deems relevant. Economic forecasters will then look at their economic growth and inflation forecasts and decide on the future outlook for interest rates.

Fiscal policy is more difficult to forecast. The government will typically provide a detailed analysis of its planned expenditure and revenue in the Budget (released in May and updated in December). Some expenditure commitments, however, like automatic stabilisers, are linked to how the economy actually unfolds. An example of an automatic stabiliser is the unemployment benefit – paid out depending on the rate of unemployment. Other areas of government expenditure are more independent of future economic performance, including health, education and justice expenditure. The government can also embark on policy changes, such as the personal tax cuts and higher rates of GST instituted in 2010.

Step 4: Forecasting the economy

Forecasting the economy is an iterative process. A forecaster will make projections based on a set of assumptions for factors that are not influenced by New Zealand economic performance, like world oil prices. The typical exogenous factors are world growth rates, world interest rates and exchange rates. Following the initial projection, interest and exchange rate assumptions may change. The forecast estimates are iterated until the projections stabilise.

This process of adjusting the drivers is part art and part science. It requires an understanding of the responsiveness of prices and policies to supply/demand imbalances. For example, monetary policy can adjust much faster than fiscal policy – the Reserve Bank has an opportunity to review interest rates every six weeks but changes in fiscal policy often take years to implement.

Some of the key relationships examined by New Zealand macro-economic forecasters are:

- **Household consumption** – This is household spending on goods and services and also holidays overseas. The main driver is household income, which is a function of employment, wages, living costs and taxes. The cost of borrowing and savings rates are also important drivers. Household spending on durable goods (e.g. cars and refrigerators) tends to be more elastic (or variable) than spending on food and services.
- **Government consumption** – Government consumption is a function of government revenue, which in turn is a function of economic growth. Government consumption tends to lag behind the economic cycle by one to two years. For example, if the economy slows, tax revenues will slow and the government will typically reduce discretionary spending, but it takes time to

change departmental budgets, which are usually set once a year in the May Budget.

- **Residential construction** – Residential construction is the construction of new homes and alterations and additions to existing homes. The key drivers for the construction cycle are the general state of the economy and the cost of borrowing. New building work needs to gain consent, so forecasters will look at data on consents for an early indication of impending construction activity. Medium- to long-term forecasts are based on the underlying requirement for homes based on population growth, changes in household size and the absorption of currently vacant homes. Interest rates and conditions in the remainder of the economy dictate how much of the underlying need for homes is actually acted on in any one period.

- **Non-residential building construction** – Each category of non-residential building construction (accommodation, social and cultural, retail, commercial, industrial, farm and other) has different drivers, but the main ones are interest rates, the general state of the economy and underlying need. For example, if there is very high office vacancy and high interest rates, then the construction of new office buildings will be weak.

- **Other business investment** – Other business investment in plant, machinery and equipment, transport equipment (often quite volatile due to the importation of aircraft), and so forth tends to be shaped by the cost of borrowing, the general state of the economy and the exchange rate. Large investments tend to be debt financed so the cost of borrowing is an important driver. If the economy is growing strongly and current plant capacity is not sufficient, then businesses will be more willing to invest. Many capital goods are imported, so when the exchange rate rises, imported goods become cheaper and many businesses take advantage of the situation.

- **Imports** – Imports are related to aggregate demand in the economy, the exchange rate and world market prices. Typically, when the economy is growing strongly it needs more imports of consumer goods for the retail sector, more capital goods for investment projects and more components (raw materials and intermediate goods) for manufacturing industries. A higher exchange rate makes imports cheaper and stimulates demand. Imports are also affected by world prices.

- **Exports** – Exports are related to domestic production, global demand, the exchange rate and global commodity prices. Forecasts of primary sector exports like dairy and meat are based primarily on production, which in turn is a function of weather and land use. Commodity prices and global demand also play important roles, but the main driver is supply. Exports of manufactured goods and tourism services are related to economic growth rates in our major trading partner economies and bilateral exchange rates. When global growth is strong, our exports flourish. Exports are further stimulated when the exchange rate is low.

- **Inflation** – The best way to think about inflation is in two parts: inflation in tradable goods prices and in non-tradable goods prices. Tradable inflation is related to global price movements (particularly oil and agricultural commodity prices) but non-tradable inflation is generated by domestic market growth pressures. If the economy is growing rapidly, then inflation will build over time, generally with a lag of around six to twelve months.

- **Interest rates** – If growth and inflation are increasing, then the OCR can be expected to rise. Longer-term interest rates like government ten-year bond yields are related to government indebtedness, the nation's foreign debt and the level of the OCR. If the OCR is high and government debt is expected to increase, longer-term borrowing costs will be forecast to rise.

- **Exchange rates** – The exchange rate is notoriously difficult to forecast because the foreign exchange market responds very quickly to a wide variety of market news. This makes the exchange rate volatile in a floating environment. The exchange rate tends to fluctuate or cycle around a long-term trend – this is said to be 'mean reverting'. In the shorter term the exchange rate will oscillate above and below this trend. These fluctuations are not random, however, and market information tends to cause some cyclical behaviour in rates. Forecasters use these patterns in their attempt to anchor short-term exchange rate forecasts.

• **Population growth** – Economists forecast population growth in two components: natural population growth and net migration. Natural population growth is births less deaths and this tends to be stable over time. Net migration is the difference between permanent and long-term arrivals and departures and this can fluctuate widely. Arrivals tend to be correlated with employment conditions in New Zealand while departures tend to be correlated with economic growth in Australia. So, when Australian economic growth is strong, net migration tends to slow in New Zealand. When net migration to New Zealand is strong, the housing market and economy tend to grow rapidly.

• **Employment and wages** – Employment and wages tend to lag behind the economic cycle. Employment tends to follow GDP growth with a lag of three to six months. This is because employers will want to be sure of a pickup or slowdown in economic growth before adjusting the number of employees. Wages tend to lag behind employment patterns by around two years. Many wage contracts are set in advance and are not reset every year, so it takes time to reflect economic conditions in wages.

Graph 9.2 shows the New Zealand Institute of Economic Research's forecasts for economic growth over the period 2011 to 2013 as at March 2011. In 2010 there was little economic growth, with lingering after-effects of the GFC. In early 2011 the recovery is slowed by economic disruption from two devastating earthquakes in Canterbury. In 2012 the recovery is expected to boom, supported by reconstruction activity in

Canterbury and a more generalised recovery in the rest of New Zealand. In 2013 growth is forecast to stabilise.

Graph 9.2 **NZIER's GDP growth forecasts**

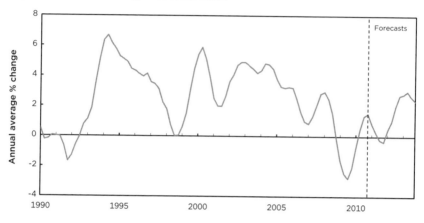

Source: Statistics NZ, NZIER
Historical GDP as per Graph 1.1, forecasts from NZIER's Quarterly Predictions publication (December 2010 edition)

This forecast of an uneven recovery path is rather different from the experience of the smooth recoveries following recessions in the early 1990s and in 1997/98. The critical factor behind this view is the current lack of growth in borrowing by households and businesses. Typically, low interest rates in a recession fuel a surge in borrowing and economic growth. However, this does not appear to be happening at present as households pay off some of the debt they have accumulated over the past decade.

The Reserve Bank is expected to raise interest rates from early 2012 and the government is expected to reduce spending. This anticipated tightening in both monetary and fiscal policy is likely to slow economic growth from late 2012. By 2012, there is expected to be a lot of pent-up demand for new homes, buildings and large-ticket items like cars and appliances. A normalisation in economic conditions will unleash this pent-up demand and lead to a strong rebound in economic growth in 2012. The catch-up in spending is expected to fade in 2013.

CONCLUSION

Forecasting is a key input into the planning process for business, government and the Reserve Bank. Forecasts are subject to error and reflect the forecaster's best estimates at any given point in time.

The starting point for a set of economic forecasts is itself uncertain, because there are significant lags in the availability of reliable current information. The basis for forecasts must be inferred from a variety of indicators.

Forecasts must take into account a wide range of market responses and future policy actions that have not actually occurred at the time forecasts are being made. Accordingly, the process is not an exact science but rather a mix of science and art.

One might be forgiven for asking whether forecasts serve any productive value to institutions and market participants. One response is that firms are continually making decisions that have repercussions far into the future. They have to 'take a view' and are accordingly reliant on forecasting exercises.

Case study 1

In this case study Professor Gary Hawke shows how technological change actually takes place. Productivity change does not arise simply as the result of an invention, but requires a series of innovations in business organisation and institutions. The case study is built around the example of the introduction of on-board refrigeration into New Zealand.

TECHNOLOGY IN THE NEW ZEALAND ECONOMY

Gary Hawke

The New Zealand economy has grown through adaptation to meet international opportunities. New Zealand incomes have depended on using New Zealand resources – labour, skills and materials – to create goods and services for which there is a consumer demand, either domestic or overseas. The level of New Zealand incomes has depended on productivity levels – output relative to inputs – which in turn have always depended on ingenuity in economising on inputs while generating output attractive to consumers.

Because New Zealand has only a small fraction of the world's population, and only a small fraction of the world's population of people with sufficient income to be able to devote time and effort to devising improvements in the use of inputs, most of the important ideas affecting the technology used in New Zealand originated overseas. However, they rarely suited New Zealand circumstances entirely, and adaptation required a great deal of ingenuity and commercial acumen.

In ordinary language, technology is often understood as an array of machinery. In economic terminology, it refers essentially to how inputs are used to produce outputs, and the scholarly literature focused on technology defines it in terms like 'a human designed means for achieving a particular end' (Dosi and Nelson, 2010, p. 55). From an economic perspective – and perhaps from other perspectives too – what is most important is the set of social, cultural and political ideas which determine what change is accommodated. Schumpeter was wise to consider new goods, new methods of production, new markets, new sources of supply, and a new form of organisation (Langlois, 2007, p. 27, n. 3, quoting the English translation of *Theory of Economic Development* (1934), p. 66). Schumpeter's distinctions of invention, innovation and diffusion are not simple but they are useful. Invention creates potential change and may generate directly the kind of satisfaction associated with any artistic creation. Innovation and diffusion are economically motivated in a more conventional sense. Consumption possibility sets are increased.

Most people would rate the most important innovation in New Zealand history as the introduction of refrigeration in the 1880s (Hawke, 1985; Hawke and Lattimore, 1999). New Zealand had developed as a part of the international economy which could supply wool competitively to industries and markets in the North Atlantic. It also had surplus sheep as they reached the end of their wool-growing utility. There was no available market for the potential meat supply. Refrigeration created such a market. It also meant that the climate which enabled New Zealand to grow grass and rear animals cheaply could support an industry which provided dairy products to markets in Europe, there previously having been no outlet for anything beyond subsistence dairying. Refrigeration was followed by a significant growth spurt which continued through the first two decades of the 20th century and created the combination of wool, meat and dairy products which dominated New Zealand exports for considerably longer.

The technology of refrigeration can be explored in a conventional manner. The preservative qualities of cold temperatures had long been known; what was added in the 19th century was engineering capability to generate low temperatures and maintain them reliably for long voyages, including through the tropics. A process which was essentially one of tinkering attracted attention in a number of places, especially Latin America and Australia, and early success with chilled meat was followed by success in refrigeration. Although the New Zealand story is sometimes told discretely, all of the essential engineering was done overseas – and as is so often the case, the role of fundamental knowledge was both minor and complex.

Physical reasons for cold being a preservative were unimportant relative to knowing that this was so. The key engineering issues concerned reliability – meat which had been frozen for only half the voyage from New Zealand to Europe had little value! Additional knowledge about the importance of air circulation developed from experience and induced gains in fundamental understanding. It also contributed to derived technologies, eventually the air conditioning of centres where large numbers of people assembled, and then to individual houses. There were technical interconnections. Refrigeration required machinery and although sailing ships could be, and were, suitably equipped – and their sails protected from inflammatory by-products of the refrigerating equipment – refrigeration was easier on steamships and eventually motor vessels. But this was a minor element in the transition from sail to steam and other technologies.

None of this technical history was at the heart of the innovation of refrigeration in New Zealand. Disposal of surplus meat was the immediate attraction for the innovation of refrigeration, but even the English could tell the difference between aged mutton and other forms of sheepmeat. Meat was best produced by raising fat lambs rather than only disposing of old sheep. Furthermore, the breeds of sheep which had been most easily acclimatised to New Zealand regions for the production of wool were not those which were best suited to production of both meat and wool – thus breeds like Romney-Southdown crosses and Lincolns replaced earlier breeds.

Dairying required even more complementary adjustment. Farm production gave way to factories where quality issues could be more controlled. That then required new ways of telling how much of the valued inputs were being supplied by individual farmers, including detecting cheats who added water to their milk. Where transport was reasonably inexpensive, milk could be conveyed to factories and turned into cheese; elsewhere, local creameries separated out the valuable milk fats and returned skim milk to producers to be used to feed pigs while the milk fats were centralised and used to produce butter. (Working all this out generated a different time sequence in exports of butter and cheese, and of both from frozen meat.) There were the same issues of determining which cattle breeds were best suited to producing dairy products in New Zealand for sale in Europe.

The produce of individual dairy farmers was necessarily aggregated to make products which could be sold in Europe. As with wool, sheep farmers could either sell their stock to local intermediaries or pay agents to convert stock to meat and convey the meat to its export market, receiving themselves the revenue it generated. The ability to sell meat 'on consignment' created a natural check on the activities of middlemen which was not available to dairy farmers. This, rather than any social difference between collectivist dairy farmers and individualistic sheep farmers, explains why co-operative dairy factories dominated the dairy industry while proprietary processors coexisted with co-operatives in the meat industry.

In either case, of course, new knowledge was needed in areas such as shipping, banking and insurance. Institutional change went much deeper. Dairy farmers soon came to need milking machinery, investment in which required more finance than could be accommodated in informal lending arrangements or standard banking facilities, but which did not require the formality of mortgages over land. This was a significant element in the development of what was initially known as 'instalment credit' and which came eventually to be known in wider contexts as hire purchase. Furthermore, new mechanisms were developed to facilitate entry into dairying and retirement of existing farmers. 'Sharemilking' divided the ownership of dairy cattle from the land on which dairying took place. A small number of standard contracts, varying the relative responsibilities of owner and sharemilker, produced the flexibility which was needed while facilitating clarity in property rights, not least for those lending money to either party.

Underlying all this change was an increase in the intensiveness with which land was used. Wool-growing could be managed on large extensive holdings with appropriate means for monitoring the work of a relatively small hired labour force. Fat-lambing and dairying both required more intensive animal husbandry and close supervision of labour which was most easily attained through owner-operator units (with less hired labour and alongside sharemilking, as already described). Most of the required reorganisation of landholdings was achieved by voluntary transactions, but even in the 19th century political rhetoric was governed by convenience rather than strict accuracy. 'Busting up the estates' was one of the great political catch cries of the late 19th century, and governments assumed power to compulsorily acquire large landholdings and reorganise them into units for intensive settlement. The powers were used mostly against corporate and overseas owners, and were sometimes used by individuals to resolve disagreements within families and partnerships – indeed, compulsory purchase was used in urban settings to settle disputes over price as inflation became significant in the early 20th century – but for present purposes, what is significant is that the institutional change needed to implement the innovation of refrigeration was wide ranging and included challenges to even such deeply embedded ideas as the sanctity of private property.*

This quick review of refrigeration is sufficient to establish that innovation cannot be equated with mechanisation. Refrigeration machinery would have had much less impact on New Zealand if it had not been accompanied by innovations in management and in institutional structures.†

---

* It helped that New Zealand society was small and had a high level of homogeneity. The analysis of voluntary institutions to overcome problems of collective choice which has recently become prominent (Ostrom, 1990) has similarities with analysis of how New Zealand governments could be agents for the settler community in Hawke (1985, Chapter 6).

† New Zealand is not unique. See Nelson and Pack (1999, especially p. 418), where it is observed that Asian growth depended not just on introduction of new technology but also on restructuring that permitted absorption of the technology – a policy regime which favoured change, an educational system which helped entrepreneurs and technicians to master and deploy new technology, and an industrial structure that enabled a new cadre to exploit the new technologies.

Mechanisation is easily seen and appreciated – more so than many aspects of innovation. Furthermore, it is a source of productivity growth that has been relatively readily available. The kind of technology which has been most susceptible to productive change is that which is 'a humanly devised means for meeting a particular end, whose workings and effectiveness are relatively uniform when employed by those skilled in the art' (Nelson, 2010, p. 9). Replicability and uniformity is the key to innovation through mechanisation. If we were seeking to maximise the pace of technological change, there is a strong case for looking to concentrate innovation in areas where mechanisation is readily possible. But if we are looking to understand where innovation has had most impact on growth, we will probably find that mechanisation was only part of the innovations which were most important and we might be willing to conjecture that the same will be true in the future.

Mechanisation relates to management of inanimate objects. Not only did New Zealand innovation depend more on how people behaved as managers and in institutional settings, but the economy depended heavily on living creatures. Even within animate objects, achieving technical change was easier with plants than with animals, and while the New Zealand economy depended on the growth of grass, it also depended on the management of sheep and cattle.

We can see the impact of this technological setting in the reaction in New Zealand to the Depression of the 1930s. Why was the response of the private sector to changes in international relative prices so weak? Innovation was weak.

New Zealand was linked to the international economy as an exporter of wool, frozen meat and dairy produce. But it was a much more complex economy than an outlying farm. It had been integrated into international services – shipping, insurance, etc. – and also in finding the cheapest way of bringing inputs into New Zealand whether as intermediate products – inputs to local services and industries – or as bulk consumer goods requiring further local processing before final consumption. This process of adaptation had been especially successful in assimilating to New Zealand conditions the basic 19th-century steam technology.

However, the inter-war economy depended a great deal on internal combustion engines and electricity. These tended to come as integrated packages. Whereas boilers, fireboxes, pistons and gears could be imported and combined with local labour and ingenuity to create steam engines, motor vehicles and electrical machinery offered less room for local activity. Eventually, motor vehicle assembly came to be a major domestic activity – and ultimately a barrier to efficient use of New Zealand resources – but the problem in the 1920s was to pay for finished imports and expensive transport. For a while, chassis and engines were imported, and local (wooden) bodies were built around them, but that did not keep pace with aerodynamic knowledge and in the later 1930s imports took the form of CKD packs – completely knocked down machines needing no further components. The Great Depression for New Zealand was a crisis of investment opportunities defined by international technology (Hawke in Gregory and Butlin, 1988). Not only was it difficult to achieve innovation in the key export sectors, it was difficult to achieve innovation resembling mechanisation too.

The relationship between innovation and research and development (R&D) is complex. New Zealand had government support for R&D related to agriculture from the late 19th century; the Department of Agriculture continued to be a major source of research and advice; and from the 1920s a Department of Scientific and Industrial Research (DSIR) was added to the mix (Galbreath, 1988).* It is no accident that the emphasis in public research was on agriculture – not so much because of the prominence of agricultural products in exports, as because of the difficulty of collective action in an industry characterised by many independent producers (albeit with a declared ideology of co-operation). The 'industrial' in the title of the DSIR showed that ambitions went beyond agriculture, but there was little clear thinking about the role of government in research.

---

* Although our conclusions are different, I benefited enormously from the research which is reported in Menzies (2008).

The relevant public institutions were reorganised in the 1980s into a policy advisory unit, Ministry of Research, Science & Technology, a funding agency, Foundation of Research Science & Technology, and a set of corporate units, Crown Research Institutes. There was no clarity over the extent to which the economic concept of public good was relied on as contrasted with a looser idea of socially useful activity funded from taxes and managed in the public sector. The prime minister has recently declared a government objective that New Zealand should participate in and contribute to international research. One might suspect that such an ambition has been present from at least the 1880s; a connection with innovation is incidental or a rationale created to justify more public funding rather than a genuine motivation.

The DSIR and other agencies generated some interesting and useful knowledge. Their historians can point to achievements in selecting wheat varieties most suited to New Zealand conditions (but wheat-growing has never been a major activity), in identifying cobalt deficiency as the cause of animal ill health in the central North Island (but after learning-by-doing had found an effective counter), in choosing trees for the development of forestry, and in countering the effects of earthquakes on buildings (unfortunately without due care in managing patent protection). But a more searching scrutiny would present conclusions like those about similar bodies in Australia where Bruce Davidson is forthright on how often knowledge came from practice and was not noticed until much later by scientists – the role of superphosphate in wheat-growing was found in the early 1880s but not mentioned at the Australian Association for the Advancement of Science until 1900 despite common references to soil fertility, and the role of clover in pastures went similarly unnoticed (Davidson in MacLeod, 1988). What was most valuable was probably the advisory service provided by people supposedly employed as researchers. It is entirely possible that the quality of the advisory services benefited from the association with a context of research and it would be an appropriate question to ask whether linking the two was the most effective and efficient mechanism for achieving that quality. Although I know of no study which bears on that question, there are works which make the case that the principal role of scientists within firms is to be information gatherers (e.g. Kealey, 1996).

For many years, no historian of technology or innovation has taken seriously the idea of a linear sequence from research to development to technology to final product. Nate Rosenberg (in Lyons et al., 2008, p. 251) has stated the consensus:

[W]e still very much exaggerate the extent to which new technology is based upon scientific research. We certainly wildly exaggerate it when we suggest, as is often suggested by the spokesmen for science in Washington, that technological change depends upon recent developments in science.

And this is a regard in which Wellington resembles Washington. Nevertheless, it remains the basis for much of our policy in the area. The notion that research has primacy and a strong claim on public expenditure can be regarded as the biggest success of a PR campaign in the 20th century, as it was how Vannevar Bush sold continuation of Manhattan Project support for scientists to the US Congress in the 1940s – fortunately, few PR consultants have an atomic bomb in their armoury.*

Nearly all economies import most of their technological development and adapt it to their local circumstances. This is simply an implication of most countries having a small share of the world's population and a small share of new ideas that inform the process of innovation. It has certainly been true of New Zealand. The archetypal New Zealand innovation is employment of overseas engineering to achieve refrigeration and major local effort in adapting breeds of livestock, husbandry methods, and institutional arrangements for finance and managing processing. We can expect the future to be similar. One of the challenges for New Zealand is to focus on innovation and stop thinking about subsidies for research. 'Commercialisation of technology' is part of the outmoded thinking.

---

* The idea of a linear progression of pure science, applied science, and economic growth was much older, going back at least to Francis Bacon (*The Advancement of Learning*, 1605), but Vannevar Bush made it dominate policy advocacy. Note the passage in the 2010 speech of President Obama to a White House gathering of scientists: 'As Vannevar Bush, who served as scientific advisor to President Franklin Roosevelt, famously said: "Basic scientific research is scientific capital".'

Innovation usually begins from generating human satisfaction and working out how to do it – at the very least there is genuine interaction between final satisfaction and perceived opportunities.

REFERENCES

Davidson, Bruce (1988). 'Developing Nature's Treasures: Agriculture and Mining in Australia'. In Roy MacLeod (ed.), *The Commonwealth of Science: ANZAAS and the Scientific Enterprise in Australasia 1888–1988*. Melbourne: Oxford University Press, pp. 274–75.

Dosi, Giovanni and Richard R. Nelson (2010). 'Technical Change and Industrial Dynamics as Evolutionary Processes'. Chapter 3 of *Handbooks in Economics*, Volume 01. Amsterdam: Elsevier, pp. 51–127.

Galbreath, R.A. (1998). *DSIR: Making Science Work for New Zealand: Themes from the History of the Department of Scientific and Industrial Research, 1926–1992*. Wellington: Victoria University Press in association with the Historical Branch, Department of Internal Affairs.

Hawke, G.R. (1985). *The Making of New Zealand*. Cambridge: Cambridge University Press.

Hawke, G.R. (1988). 'Depression and Recovery in New Zealand'. In R.G. Gregory and N.G. Butlin (eds), *Recovery from the Depression: Australia and the World Economy in the 1930s*. Cambridge: Cambridge University Press, pp. 113–34.

Hawke, Gary and Ralph Lattimore (1999). *Visionaries, Farmers and Markets: An Economic History of New Zealand Agriculture*. NZ Trade Consortium Working Paper No. 1. Wellington: NZIER.

Kealey, T. (1996). *The Economic Laws of Scientific Research*. London: Macmillan.

Langlois, Richard N. (2007). *The Dynamics of Industrial Capitalism: Schumpeter, Chandler, and the New Economy*. London and New York: Routledge, The Graz Schumpeter Lectures.

Lyons, John, S., Louis P. Cain and Samuel H. Williamson (2008). *Reflections on the Cliometric Revolution: Conversations with Economic Historians*. London and New York: Routledge Explorations in Economic History.

Menzies, Malcolm Bruce (2008). 'Recognising Scientific Entrepreneurship in New Zealand'. PhD thesis, Victoria University of Wellington.

Nelson, R.R. and H. Pack (1999). 'The Asian Miracle and Economic Theory'. *Economic Journal* 109, pp. 416–36.

Nelson, Richard R. (2010). 'The Moon and the Ghetto Revisited'. http://nickfest.freeman-centre.ac.uk/conference-program/r-nelson_the-moon-and-the-ghetto-revisited.pdf

Ostrom, Elinor (1990). *Governing the Commons: The Evolution of Institutions for Collective Action*. Cambridge: Cambridge University Press.

Case study 2

In this case study Professor Philip McCann canvasses an emerging area of economic thinking, economic geography. He illustrates how economic geography and government shape the regions of an economy using Auckland and New Zealand as an example.

CITIES AND GLOBALISATION: IS AUCKLAND SPECIAL?

Philip McCann

This case study sketches out the major issues relating to the current era of globalisation and how these recent global technological and institutional changes have impacted on the economic geography of the New Zealand economy. To begin with, we consider these issues from a longer-term perspective and then identify how the recent changes have impacted on internal and external aspects of the New Zealand economy. The first section considers some of the major changes to the New Zealand economy that have taken place over the last century of globalisation, and this allows us to set the recent globalisation changes in context. Following sections discuss such changes from the perspective of economic geography. The final section interprets these observations in light of the particular characteristics of the contemporary New Zealand economy.

The New Zealand economy and globalisation

During the six decades following the Treaty of Waitangi, New Zealand was the fastest-growing economy in the world. Indeed, by the year 1914, on the eve of World War I, in terms of wealth per person – or more precisely gross domestic product (GDP) per capita – New Zealand was one of the world's richest countries. During the 19th and early 20th centuries New Zealand had emerged as an agricultural producer and exporter, whose exports were focused originally on wood, gum, flax and wool, and then with the advent of refrigeration, increasingly also on meat exports. During the 20th century, New Zealand's exports diversified, and as well as an increasing scale of meat exports, the country also increasingly shifted towards dairy exports, as well as an expanding range of agricultural and environmental goods and services, including tourism.

During the early years of its rapid growth, spanning more or less the period between the mid-19th century and first half of the 20th century, New Zealand's exports were primarily bound for the UK market. In exchange, New Zealand imported manufactured goods from the United Kingdom. The UK was also the major source of finance capital for New Zealand's large-scale infrastructure investment, in sectors such as the railways, mining, and the port and harbour facilities. This pattern of trade between New Zealand and the UK reflected a more general trade within the British Empire and Commonwealth system. For more than a century, the UK had maintained a sophisticated, highly integrated and highly deregulated set of bilateral trade relationships with each of its dominions – namely, Canada, New Zealand, Australia and South Africa.

These dense bilateral flows of goods and commodities between the UK and each of its four individual dominions were also mirrored in terms of flows of people. However, there were also major differences, in that the flows of people were largely one-way, in the sense that they were away from the UK. The largely unrestricted mobility between the five countries resulted in large global flows of people within this international system, most of whom emerged from the UK – which was by far the most densely populated of the five and the most focused on producing manufacturing goods – and settled in the four countries focused more on the production of extractive and agricultural goods. Migrants into New Zealand and Australia also emanated from other countries as well, and in the case of New Zealand in particular, large flows of people arrived from Ireland, China, Eastern Europe and the Netherlands, as well as from other Pacific nations.

New Zealand's trade with Australia was small in comparison with its trade with the UK, and once again this reflected a more general pattern in which the trade between each of the four dominions was small. Indeed, even by the late 1960s, the proportion of New Zealand's exports accounted for by Australia was little more than 5 per cent. From the 1960s onwards, however, the trade position and role of the New Zealand economy began to change.

During the 1950s and 1960s, many of the advanced and industrial economies, which had been ravaged by the Second World War, started to revive. From the late 1960s onwards, many of the other rich countries started to catch up with New Zealand. It was during this period of the second half of the 20th century that the long-term historical trends of globalisation slowly started to regain their momentum, and as a trading nation these trends had major impacts on the New Zealand economy.

Globalisation processes have been in train for approximately four centuries, driven at each stage by different technological and political developments. Yet, strangely, much of the 20th century can be seen as an exception to these long-run processes. The catastrophes of the two world wars and the inter-war Depression of the 1930s led to massive contractions of global trade and international investment. The reconstruction era after World War II was characterised by restrictions on the international movement of money, under what became known as the Bretton Woods system, named after the location in New Hampshire, United States, where the agreement was devised in 1944. The Bretton Woods system insulated individual national economies from many aspects of the long-run historical globalisation processes, and this was successful for more than a quarter of a century. During the 1970s and 1980s the major economies' markets started to become increasingly integrated once again, as global international financial flows accelerated and newly emerging countries such as Japan and South Korea started to dominate many manufacturing sectors.

From the 1950s, New Zealand had been moving slowly towards a more liberal economic and financial regime. It was a stop-start affair until 1984 when government took the opportunity of a foreign exchange crisis to undertake far-reaching free-market reforms. These reforms took place almost continually from 1984 to 1997. During this thirteen-year period New Zealand was transformed from a highly regulated mixed economy, whose economic structure had been constructed during the era of the British Commonwealth trading system described above, to a highly deregulated free-market economy, engaging with the whole global economy. These reforms coincided, or were influenced by, the fundamental changes in the global economy that occurred within a period of less than five years, between the end of the 1980s and the early 1990s, and these changes were both technological and institutional in nature.

In terms of technological changes, the 1970s and 1980s saw the rapid rise in modern transportation and communications technologies. New forms of freight haulage developed around the principles of containerisation, roll-on roll-off (RO-RO) technologies, and advances in global positioning system (GPS) technologies facilitated by satellite systems. At the same time, air transportation became ever more affordable as technological improvements were associated with the development of the Boeing 747 jumbo jet, along with massive deregulations in global transportation systems and networks. Transportation costs fell by more than 95 per cent during the 20th century. Meanwhile, the 1980s also saw the emergence of widespread use of computing in business, and the emergence of the first generation of mobile telephone technologies. However, it was the advent of the internet in 1991, following the invention of the hypertext transfer protocol (http) by Tim Berners-Lee, which for the first time allowed these diverse technologies to become increasingly integrated. Information and communications technologies (ICTs), as we nowadays understand them, are therefore only a very recent phenomenon, and are really the product of merging during the early 1990s of computing and telecommunications technologies.

At the same time as these fundamental global technological changes were taking place, equally fundamental global institutional changes were occurring. The fall of the Berlin Wall in 1989, the start of the market reforms in China after 1979, the 1991 industrial reforms in Indonesia, the readmittance of South Africa to the global community after the release of Nelson Mandela in 1990, the 1991 deregulation and reforms in India, and the flotation of the new Brazilian currency, the real, in 1994, together brought some 1.5 billion new workers into the global economy between 1989 and 1994. At the same time, the creation of the European Union single market in 1992 and the formation of the North American Free Trade Agreement (NAFTA) in 1994, and further integrating developments in the South and East Asia region, all led to the development of three super-regional areas of economic integration, built around enormous internal markets and free-trade areas. The development of these three massive internal markets and free-trade areas – namely, the EU, NAFTA and South and East Asia – have altered the geography of international trade and investment, such that it now is becoming increasingly centred on these three zones.

Finally, in response to the commercial opportunities afforded by these technological and institutional changes, over the last two decades we have also witnessed an enormous increase in corporate organisational changes, whereby multinational firms outsource and offshore increasing numbers and types of economic activities to the newly emerging economies. Multinationals are rapidly increasing their presence and role in the global economy to the extent that, in many ways, multinationalism is nowadays more important in driving globalisation than international trade.

Economic geography and globalisation
Over the last two decades of globalisation one of the major outcomes of these technological, institutional and corporate organisation changes is that the economic geography of the world economy has changed fundamentally. In particular, the fact that information and communications technologies are now widespread across the globe has led many observers to assume that the world is becoming 'flat', in the sense that places are becoming ever more accessible and therefore even. With such technologies, it doesn't matter where you are in the world.

However, while certain types of standardised and routine activities can easily be outsourced and offshored with the help of ICTs, many knowledge-intensive activities require ever more face-to-face contact, even when ICTs are being used intensively. Ask yourself how many people you interact with every week using cell phones, email and Facebook, and compare the number of these people who live in the same city as you with those who live in faraway countries. You will see that most people you communicate with using ICTs are the same ones who you regularly communicate with face to face. This is also true for business activities. People in business also interact the most, using ICTs, with the same people with whom they interact face to face. The reason is that as we move to a knowledge-intensive service-driven economy, the costs of doing business across space are actually increasing, as our requirements for face-to-face contact are also increasing. This is not true for low knowledge-intensive activities, many of which nowadays do not require much face-to-face contact, and can therefore easily be outsourced or offshored. In reality, the advent of ICTs has not made the world flat or more even, but rather has made it increasingly uneven, increasingly 'spiky'.

There are two major aspects to this unevenness. First, what economic geographers call 'agglomeration economies' appear to be more important than ever. Economic activity appears to be increasingly associated with cities, and this is particularly true for high knowledge-intensive activities. Moreover, certain types of cities appear to play a more important role in modern globalisation, and we call these places 'global cities'. They are characterised by high numbers of highly educated and skilled workers undertaking highly paid jobs, many of which relate to knowledge activities and multinational roles. Secondly, all forms of trade and investment appear to be increasingly concentrated in regions which are comprised of groups of countries, such as the EU, NAFTA and South and East Asia, and all forms of international activity appear to be focused on neighbouring and adjacent countries. Globalisation, therefore, appears to be rather more like global regionalism in nature, rather than something which is genuinely international. Most multinational firms spend the majority of their time and effort engaging with nearby countries, rather than those on the other side of the world.

Countries which are growing rapidly in the modern era of globalisation appear to be those which benefit from both agglomeration economies, and particularly those associated with global cities, and also from the presence of wide and dense networks of major multinational firms with access to major markets. Many countries are struggling in the global marketplace. There is much evidence to suggest that this difficulty is usually related to the problems of achieving economies of scale or developing major cities. These problems also appear to be related to achieving accessibility to major markets. Being a small country with a small domestic market, but which is also adjacent to large markets, allows that country to achieve these economies of scale. Being both small and an isolated economy limits the ability of a country to achieve economies of scale.

The national characteristics of New Zealand are rather different to those of many other economies. For an advanced industrialised country it has a very particular mixture of low population scale and low population density, high levels of urbanisation but with very small cities, high levels of international openness, the most extreme geographical isolation and the lowest market accessibility of any developed country, a very high reliance on land-based exports, and the lowest level of export diversity of any advanced economy. Australia exhibits similar geographical characteristics to New Zealand, although Australia is a larger and a more diverse economy. There are strong grounds for believing that in the current era of globalisation these features pose major challenges for New Zealand. Its responses to these challenges also help to explain many of the emerging features of the domestic New Zealand economy, most notably the increasingly important role played by Auckland.

Auckland is continuing to grow rapidly, even though it is already by far the largest city in New Zealand, and also the most expensive city in which to live, with the longest commuting times and largest traffic jams. So why are more people moving to live and work in Auckland? The answer is that Auckland is New Zealand's 'global city'. Auckland is the location of New Zealand's largest concentration of knowledge-intensive activities and occupations, and also the types of jobs which are associated with multinational operations and global engagement. Moreover, following the arguments above, not only is Auckland New Zealand's global city, and therefore New Zealand's major access point or gateway to the global economy, but also most of Auckland's economic connections are with Australia's global cities, notably Sydney and Melbourne. Knowledge-intensive occupations and activities undertaken by firms in Auckland primarily involve engagement with firms located in these Australian cities.

What we see here in New Zealand is typical of the patterns we observe in other parts of the world, where global cities are increasingly dominated by knowledge-intensive jobs and involve operations and activities engaging with other global cities in the same parts of the world. The advent of Closer Economic Relations (CER) between Australia and New Zealand in the early 1980s promoted such engagement, and the globalisation processes we have already described simply built on these institutional changes. Global regionalism in this part of the world means Australia-New Zealand; and the role played by global cities means Sydney and Melbourne in Australia and Auckland in New Zealand.

To summarise to this point, the future role of Auckland in the New Zealand economy, or alternatively the long-term relationship between the New Zealand economy and that of Australia, is being driven by the regional globalisation forces discussed above. These forces may be summarised as follows.

As economies increasingly shift toward the production of services, rather than manufactured goods, ever-expanding opportunities for face-to-face interaction become increasingly important. The largest city provides more opportunities for these industries, and therefore as the share of services in the economy increases, so does the size of the largest city.

The arguments imply that as globalisation proceeds, the differences between the largest city and relatively smaller cities will tend to increase. This is not to say that all major cities will increase relative to smaller cities in all cases. Different cities are dominated by different industries and technologies, and these industries and technologies themselves rise and fall over time, irrespective of what is going on in any particular city. However, as a general pattern, these forces are sufficient to explain why Auckland is still growing, becoming more densely populated, and increasingly dominated by knowledge-intensive service activities. Similarly, the theory explains why the major capital cities of each Australian state are also growing relative to the smaller cities in their respective states. Finally, the same arguments capture most of the features of the relationship between Sydney and Auckland and, by implication, Australia and New Zealand.

Cities, globalisation and the New Zealand economy
The arguments and evidence presented here therefore suggest that economic geography forces are operating on the New Zealand economy both internationally and internally.

The international aspects of economic geography, the most recent phase of globalisation, rather than making the world flatter and therefore less isolated, place more weight on accessibility and accordingly have made geographical proximity more important and isolation more problematic. New Zealand is a geographically isolated economy and evidence for the role that geography plays on economic performance comes from the World Bank (2009) and the OECD (2008a, b), both of which have argued that the adverse effects of geographical isolation on productivity are greater in the case of New Zealand and Australia than for any other advanced economy. OECD (2008a, b) estimates for both countries suggest that distance reduces New Zealand's worker productivity by more than 10 per cent, and IMF (2004) estimations also imply that some 50 per cent of the labour productivity gap between New Zealand and the average for other rich economies can be attributed to geography alone.

However, geographical isolation may not be the whole story. One major advantage that larger countries such as Australia have over New Zealand is the widespread existence of economies of scale (NZIER, 2006). Indeed, further estimations (OECD, 2008b) suggest that Australia's scale more than compensates for the adverse effects of distance, whereas in the case of New Zealand the small country effect means that the productivity gap with other rich countries increases to more than 14 per cent.

These complex economic geography forces are also operating internally within New Zealand. If we examine the internal spatial structure of the country, the highest per capita productivity region is Auckland – the largest city and agglomeration of New Zealand. The region accounts for approximately 33 per cent of the population and just over 40 per cent of New Zealand's output. During the decade spanning 1991 to 2001, Auckland was New Zealand's second-fastest-growing major labour market area, after Tauranga, and provisional 2006 Census estimates indicate that the regional area with the highest growth rate during the more recent period of 2001 to 2006 was also Auckland. Not surprisingly, private sector wages are also the highest in Auckland and are increasing. Auckland has New Zealand's highest number of headquarter functions associated with the world's major companies, and evidence also suggests that increasing numbers of New Zealand corporate headquarter functions are moving out of Wellington and into Auckland. These observations all point to the contemporary importance of large city agglomeration within the New Zealand economy itself.

However, Auckland is currently not a major export location of its own accord, with an export to GDP ratio which is actually below that of other New Zealand regions (McCann, 2009). Rather, following our earlier discussion of globalisation, within the New Zealand economy, Auckland acts as a knowledge conduit through which exports and imports of all New Zealand's sectors, produced in all regions, can be facilitated. Auckland can be considered to be the dominant location where New Zealand connects with the rest of the global marketplace.

Public policy therefore needs to ensure that the growth of Auckland proceeds as smoothly as possible. The recent move towards a simpler and more integrated 'Super City' organisational structure should facilitate the planning of the appropriate infrastructure and the land-use policies required to help the city grow in an organised and appropriate manner. However, does this imply that all economic policy in New

Zealand should focus mainly on promoting Auckland? It is not quite that straightforward, because New Zealand's exports are dominated by products and services produced by other parts of the country. (Auckland is different from London in this regard.) The export specialisation of New Zealand means that the country's exports will still continue to be dominated by agriculture and tourism for decades to come, and these exports will be driven by the other New Zealand regions. Therefore, from a policy perspective, a major focus should be on finding ways to upgrade the connectivity of Auckland to the rest of the country. Such policies might focus on the domestic air-transportation system, as well as on the upgrading and redirecting of New Zealand's biosciences infrastructure into more competitive and advanced exports, embodying ever more knowledge-intensive inputs. Further discussions on these points can be found in McCann (2009).

REFERENCES

IMF (2004). *New Zealand: Selected Issues*. IMF Country Report No. 04/127. Washington, DC: International Monetary Fund.
McCann, P. (2009). 'Economic Geography, Globalisation and New Zealand's Productivity Paradox'. *New Zealand Economic Papers* 43(3), pp. 279–314.
NZIER (2006). *The New Zealand-Australian Income Differential*. Working Paper 2006/05. Wellington: NZIER.
OECD (2008a). *Economic Policy Reforms: Going for Growth*. Paris: OECD.
OECD (2008b). *The Contribution of Economic Geography to GDP per Capita*. Economics Department Working Paper. Paris: OECD.
World Bank (2009). *Reshaping Economic Geography: World Development Report*. Washington, DC: The World Bank.

Further resources

The reference list given below contains works that were used in the preparation of this book. Those readers interested in exploring New Zealand's economic history from the time of European settlement might begin with Hawke (1985), *The Making of New Zealand*. Economic histories concentrating on the post-World War II period include *Trade, Growth and Anxiety* by Harvey Franklin, *The Rake's Progress* by John Gould, *In Stormy Seas* by Brian Easton, *The New Zealand Macroeconomy* by Paul Dalziel and Ralph Lattimore, and the articles mentioned in the preface.

In 2007 the Ministry of Economic Development began a useful publication series that includes a wide range of economic indicators. A second edition was published earlier this year, MED (2011).

Abelson, Peter (2003). *Public Economics: Principles and Practice*. Sydney: Applied Economics.

Anderson, Kym and Will Martin (2007). *Distortions to Agricultural Incentives in Asia*. Agricultural Distortions Working Paper 59. Washington, DC: The World Bank.

Anderson, Kym, Ralph Lattimore, Peter Lloyd and Donald MacLaren (2009). 'Australia and New Zealand'. Chapter 5 in Kym Anderson (ed.), *Distortions to Agricultural Incentives: A Global Perspective 1955–2007*. Palgrave Macmillan and The World Bank.

Arrow, Kenneth J. (1962). 'The economic implications of learning by doing'. *Review of Economic Studies* 29, pp. 155–73.

Belich, James (2001). *Paradise Reforged: A History of the New Zealanders from the 1880s to the Year 2000*. Auckland: Allen Lane.

Bell, Matthew, Gary Blick, Oscar Parkin, Paul Rodway and Polly Vowles (2010). *Challenges and Choices: Modelling New Zealand's Long-term Fiscal Position*. Working Paper 10/01. Wellington: New Zealand Treasury.

Bhagwati, Jagdish (2008a). Speech to the Oxford Forum, Oxford University, May.

Bhagwati, Jagdish (2008b). *Termites in the Trading System*. Oxford: Oxford University Press.

Bollard, Alan with Sarah Gaitanas (2010). *Crisis: One Central Bank Governor and the Global Financial Collapse*. Auckland: Auckland University Press.

Borchert, Ingo and Aaditya Mattoo (2009). *The Crisis-Resilience of Services Trade*. Working Paper series 4917. Washington, DC: The World Bank.

Bordo, Michael (2009). *Global shocks, Global Financial Crises: How Can Small Open Economies like New Zealand Protect Themselves? An Historical Perspective*. New Zealand, July 2009. http://sites.google.com/site/michaelbordo/home32

Claus, Iris, Ralph Lattimore, Trinh Le and Adolf Stroombergen (2009). *Progress and Puzzles: Long-term structural change in the New Zealand economy, 1953–2006*. Working Paper 2009/6. Wellington: NZIER.

Coase, Ronald (1937). 'The Nature of the Firm'. *Economica* NS4, pp. 386–405.

Coyle, William, Mark Gehlhar, Thomas Hertel, Zhi Wang and Wusheng Yu (1998). 'Understanding the Determinants of Structural Change in World Food Markets'. *American Journal of Agricultural Economics* 80(5), pp. 1051–61.

Cranfield, John, Thomas Hertel, James Eales and Paul Preckel (1998). 'Changes in the Structure of Global Food Demand'. *American Journal of Agricultural Economics* 80(5), pp. 1042–50.

Dalziel, Paul and Ralph Lattimore (2004). *The New Zealand Macroeconomy*, 5th edn. Melbourne: Oxford University Press.

Delgardo, Christopher, Mark Rosegrant, Henning Steinfeld, Simeon Ehui and Claude Courbois (1999). *Livestock to 2020: The Next Food Revolution*. Washington, DC: International Food Policy Research Institute.

Dicken, Peter (2003). *Global Shift: Reshaping the Global Economic Map in the 21st Century*. London: Sage.

Dimaranan, Betins, Elena Ianchovichina and Will Martin (2007). 'Competing with Giants: Who Wins, Who Loses?' Chapter 3 in Winters and Yusuf (2007), op. cit.

Easton, Brian (1997). *In Stormy Seas: The Post-War New Zealand Economy*. Dunedin: Otago University Press.

Ferguson, Niall (2008). *The Ascent of Money*. New York: Allen Lane.

Franklin, Harvey (1978). *Trade, Growth and Anxiety*. Wellington: Methuen.

Gibson, John (2009). 'The Rising Public Sector Pay Premium in the New Zealand Labour Market'. *New Zealand Economic Papers* 43(3), pp. 255–61.

Gould, John (1982). *The Rake's Progress*. Auckland: Hodder & Stoughton.

Growth Commission (2008). *The Growth Report: Strategies for Sustained Growth and Inclusive Development*. Washington, DC: The World Bank.

Grubel, Hubert and Peter Lloyd (1975). *Intra-industry Trade*. London: Macmillan.

Hawke, Gary (1985). *The Making of New Zealand*. Cambridge: Cambridge University Press.

Kee, H.L., A. Nicita and M. Olarreaga (2006). *Estimating trade restrictiveness indices*. Policy Research Working Paper 3840. Washington, DC: The World Bank.

Krugman, Paul (1979). 'Increasing Returns, Monopolistic Competition and International Trade'. *Journal of International Economics* 9, pp. 469–79.

Krugman, Paul (2009). 'The Increasing Returns Revolution in Trade and Geography'. *American Economic Review* 99(3), pp. 561–71.

Lattimore, Ralph (1999). *Is Livestock a Sunset Industry?* Paper presented to the Joint AWAC-ANZCCART Conference (Royal Society of New Zealand), Wellington, 18 November 1999.

Lattimore, Ralph (2008). *NZ exports – more diverse than commonly thought*. NZIER Insight 06/2009. Wellington: NZIER.

Lattimore, Ralph, Javier Reyes and Chris Schilling (2009). *New Zealand's role in world food networks*. Discussion Paper. Wellington: NZIER.

Leamer, Edward E. (2007). 'A Flat World, a Level Playing Field, a Small World After All, or None of the Above?' A review of Thomas L. Friedman's *The World is Flat. Journal of Economic Literature*, March, pp. 83–126.

Love, Patrick and Ralph Lattimore (2009). *International Trade: Free, Fair and Open?* OECD Insights series. Paris: OECD.

McCann, Philip (2009). 'Economic Geography, Globalisation and New Zealand's Productivity Paradox'. *New Zealand Economic Papers* 43(3), pp. 279–314.

McDermott, John and Viv Hall. *A Quarterly Post-World War II Real GDP Series for New*

Zealand. RBNZ Discusssion Paper, DP2009/12.

Maddison, A. (2003). *The World Economy: Historical Statistics.* Paris: OECD Development Centre.

MED (2007). *Economic Development Indicators 2007.* Wellington: Ministry of Economic Development with the Treasury and Statistics New Zealand.

MED (2011). *Economic Development Indicators 2011.* Wellington: Ministry of Economic Development with the Treasury and Statistics New Zealand.

Porter, Michael E. (1990). *The Competitive Advantage of Nations.* New York: Free Press.

Rae, David and Marte Sollie (2008). *Globalisation and the European Union: Which countries are best placed to cope?* Economics Department Working Paper No. 586. Paris: OECD.

Rayner, Anthony and Ralph Lattimore (1991). 'New Zealand'. In Demetris Papageorgiou, Michael Michaely and Armeane Choksi (eds), *Liberalizing Foreign Trade.* Cambridge, Mass.: Blackwell.

Reddell, Michael and Cathy Sleeman (2008). 'Some perspectives on past recessions'. *Reserve Bank of New Zealand Bulletin* 71(2), pp. 5–21.

Reinhart, Carmen and Kenneth Rogoff (2008). *This Time is Different: A Panoramic View of Eight Centuries of Financial Crises.* Working Paper 13882. Cambridge, Mass.: NBER. http://www.economics.harvard.edu/files/faculty/51_This_Time_Is_Different.pdf

Reyes, Javier, Martina Garcia and Ralph Lattimore (2009). 'The New International Economic Order and Trade Architecture'. *Spatial Economic Analysis*, March, pp. 73–102.

Safadi, Raed and Ralph Lattimore (eds) (2008). *Globalisation and Emerging Economies: Brazil, Russia, India, Indonesia, China and South Africa.* Paris: OECD.

Sally, Razeen (2008). *Globalisation and the Political Economy of Trade Liberalisation in the BRIICS.* Chapter 4 in Safadi and Lattimore, op. cit.

Seale, James, Jr, Anita Regmi and Jason Bernstein (2003). 'International Evidence on Food Consumption Patterns'. *Technical Bulletins* 33580. United States Department of Agriculture, Economic Research Service.

Statistics New Zealand (2010). *Industry Productivity Statistics 1978–2008.* Wellington: Statistics New Zealand.

Treasury (2009). *International Connections and Productivity: Making Globalisation Work for New Zealand.* Treasury Productivity Paper 09/01. http://www.treasury.govt.nz/publications/research-policy/tprp/09-01

Vernon, Raymond (1966). 'International Investment and International Trade in the Product Cycle'. *Quarterly Journal of Economics* 80(2), pp. 190–207.

Winters, Alan and Shahid Yusuf (2007). *Dancing with Giants: China, India and the Global Economy.* Washington, DC: The World Bank.

FURTHER RESOURCES

Index

Authors

Ralph Lattimore was a professor of economics at the University of British Columbia and Lincoln University for many years before working for the New Zealand Institute of Economic Research and then the OECD. He has worked as a consulting economist in over 20 countries. As well as the five publications listed in the further reading section of this book, and numerous journal articles, he is author with Brian Silverstone and Alan Bollard of *A Study of Economic Reform: The Case of New Zealand* (North-Holland, 1996). Ralph may be contacted at 25 Sunview Heights, RD1 Richmond 7081, New Zealand, or Ralph. Lattimore@yahoo.com.

Shamubeel Eaqub has been a private sector economist since 2001 in New Zealand and Australia and is now the principal economist at the New Zealand Institute of Economic Research. He is a regular commentator in the media and is widely called upon by businesses for economic advice. He may be reached at the New Zealand Institute of Economic Research, Wellington, New Zealand, or at Shamubeel.Eaqub@nzier.org.nz.

Gary Hawke is professor emeritus at Victoria University of Wellington and senior fellow at the New Zealand Institute of Economic Research. He joined the staff of Victoria University of Wellington in 1968, and retired as head of the School of Government and professor of economic history in 2008. He was a visiting fellow at Stanford University in the United States, All Souls' College, Oxford in the United Kingdom, at the Australian National University in Australia, and with a number of institutions in Japan. He was Tawney Lecturer for the Economic History Society in the UK in 1978, and in 1998 in New Zealand he was awarded the NZIER-Qantas Prize in Economics. He is a fellow of the Royal Society of New Zealand, distinguished fellow of the New Zealand Association of Economists and fellow of the Institute of Public Administration of New Zealand. He is a Companion of the New Zealand Order of Merit.

Philip McCann holds the University of Groningen Endowed Chair of Economic Geography. He is one of the most highly cited and widely recognised economic geographers and spatial economists of his generation. He is also professor of economics in the Department of Economics at the University of Waikato, New Zealand, and formerly professor of urban and regional economics in the Department of Economics, at the University of Reading, UK. Professor Philip McCann is a special adviser to Johannes Hahn, the European Commissioner for Regional Policy.